GENDERED BODIES AND PUBLIC SCRUTINY

GENDERED BODIES AND PUBLIC SCRUTINY

Women's Stories of Staring, Strangers, and Fierce Resistance

Victoria Kannen

Illustrated by Damian Mellin

WOMEN'S PRESS

Toronto | Vancouver

Gendered Bodies and Public Scrutiny: Women's Stories of Staring,
Strangers, and Fierce Resistance
Victoria Kannen

First published in 2021 by
Women's Press, an imprint of CSP Books Inc.
425 Adelaide Street West, Suite 200
Toronto, Ontario
M5V 3C1

www.womenspress.ca

Library and Archives Canada Cataloguing in Publication

Title: Gendered bodies and public scrutiny : women's stories of staring, strangers, and fierce resistance / Victoria Kannen ; illustrated by Damian Mellin.
Names: Kannen, Victoria, 1981- author. | Mellin, Damian, illustrator.
Description: Includes bibliographical references.
Identifiers: Canadiana (print) 20210336668 | Canadiana (ebook) 20210336714 |
ISBN 9780889616295 (softcover) | ISBN 9780889616301 (PDF) |
ISBN 9780889616318 (EPUB)
Subjects: LCSH: Human body—Social aspects. | LCSH: Women—Public opinion. |
LCSH: Human body—Public opinion. | LCSH: Women—Physiology. | LCSH:
Women—Social conditions. | LCSH: Women—Psychology.
Classification: LCC HQ1206 .K36 2021 | DDC 305.42—dc23

Cover image and design by Damian Mellin
Page layout by S4Carlisle Publishing Services

21 22 23 24 25   5 4 3 2 1

Printed and bound in Ontario, Canada

Canada

Dedication

For my mother, Christina. Thank you for showing me how to be a strong and loving woman, and to never settle for a life that is just "fine."

Contents

Acknowledgements

This book came together because of so many wonderful people. The seven participants, whose actual names I hold close, shared so much with me: their time, intimate stories, laughter, and support. I can't imagine what this book would have become without each one of them. Damian Mellin was a joy to have as the illustrator. We didn't know each other before this project, and I am so thankful that he came along on this journey. This book looks and feels the way it does because of his very cool involvement. Thanks to Lizzie Di Giacomo, Ryan Pidhayny, and all the folks from Women's Press for their overwhelming support and patience through this creation. 2020 was such a bizarre time to embark on a project like this, and they were unwavering in their commitment to *Gendered Bodies and Public Scrutiny* throughout this whole process. The four anonymous peer reviewers were also invaluable in their support of my work. Their engaging questions and comments encouraged me to push this work even further. I am indebted to Lex Dyer for her thoughts, notes, and questions on the draft of the book. Mostly, though, I am thankful to her for always loving and supporting me. Thanks to Penelope, Zoe, and Ian, for making me laugh, listening to me ramble, and always asking amazing questions about whatever projects I am working on. Lastly, I want to make it clear that this book would not exist if not for my partner in this life, Aaron. His love, encouragement, curiosity, and unyielding belief in me are what inspired me to pursue this project in the first place. I am grateful for him, every day.

CHAPTER 1

Inspiring Awe, Feeling Odd

Our bodies have stories. These stories help define *who* we are and *how* we are with other people. Some bodies foster awe—creating wonder, curiosity, admiration, and engagement—while other bodies are read as odd—those that are extraordinary spectacles, and may make others uncomfortable and anxious. It is most often the case that a body that inspires awe is also a body made to feel odd. This book explores the experiences of self-identified women and the ways their bodies can be interpreted in the public and private spaces of society. There are many concepts to work through here: gender, race, space, the body itself, and so on. Working through these concepts will also be an aim of this book—to help clarify what can be meant by these words, why they matter, and how they can relate to your own experiences.

I wanted to write this book because we can read theories of bodies, but they are often too abstract. We can see images of bodies, particularly those of women, but they can be too separate from their story to be meaningful to us. I wanted to combine story, interpretation, representation, and theory to demonstrate the ways that we can make sense of gendered bodies in a more holistic way. I was also encouraged to write this book because, many years ago, I realized that my life—and the lives of so many women—orbit around this quote: "What you look like, rather than who you are, often determines how people respond to you" (Garland-Thomson 2009, 34). Since then, my teaching, research, and writing have focused on identities, social power, and what it means to appear to one another.

The stories told in this book are what I call **body stories**. We all have them. You. Me. Everyone. My story is included (see Chapter 5) because, like the other seven body stories in this book, we have bodies that inspire awe from those who see us *and* we have all been placed in categories that relegate us to "odd"—amongst other such labels. Our stories are unique to us, but you can form a relationship to these stories in some way. You will also interpret our stories in various ways, and that is part of the goal. Our bodies are interpreted by others constantly— these tellings are also interpretations and will be further interpreted by you. But the aim of this book is to have you consider the construction of appearances, the meanings that everyone's body gives off, the role of others in shaping how we come to think of ourselves, and what it means to inspire awe and feel odd simultaneously. This is not a history book, nor a comprehensive theory book. This is a book about bodies and interpretations (both through language and art) of the stories of extraordinary women.

I have prioritized the role of storytelling in this book because I see it as a way to give power to the participants, so that they can create their own plot lines for their body stories. While I asked them questions in our discussions, my questions were very open and allowed each person to navigate what was important to them about their embodied selves. As you will see, telling the stories of our bodies is personal, challenging, conflicting, and, often, liberating.

These people told their body stories for you to read, imagine, learn from, interpret, and reflect on. I will use their words and their experiences throughout and explore them alongside theories of bodies and identities in order to illuminate the connections and concepts that fuel their body stories. Their stories have also been imagined through art— Damian Mellin created art pieces based not on what the seven participants looked like (as he did not see them), but rather from how they told their stories. They are interpretations and representations. The purpose of these three key elements—story, art, and theory—is to convey the various ways that our embodiments can be explored in academic settings (and beyond).

You may have noticed that I am speaking to you directly—rather than keeping my language neutral. I also use "we" and, at times, "our" to discuss bodies and social experience. I recognize that this can be disarming for some of you; our experiences are not necessarily shared, and there are power imbalances between all of us that make any assumptions of a collective potentially problematic. The reason for the "we" is simple—we all have a body and, to some extent, are our bodies. This is fact.

While I am writing this book, we are going through an extraordinary and challenging time, globally. The COVID-19 pandemic is in full swing, and many of us have now shifted the ways our bodies are presented in public due to wearing masks and being quite mindful of the health of our bodies and their proximity to others, and—for many of us—our public interactions now occur from home over various video-conferencing platforms. I feel that the time for a book on the malleability and socially constructed nature of our bodies has never been more relevant. Comments on our bodies are taking on new forms, policing the bodies of other people has never been more explicit, and the blurring of boundaries between private and public spaces is in a state of unprecedented flux.

Having said that, we do not all share the same experiences. The differences between our lives are many, and they will be made clear throughout this book, but we *do* share in the experience of having bodies and experiencing those bodies in relation to other people. The aim of this work is to expose you, the reader, to new ideas and questions. Before we get too far in, then, there are some fundamental ideas that we need to work through. It is important to outline upfront the key approaches to this book, so that you know what to expect. The body and its identities, such as gender, race, and disability, as well as theories of appearing and staring will be explored in this chapter to help set the stage for what you will be exposed to throughout the book. The chapter will then conclude with a general overview of what you can expect from the rest of the book.

TERMS AND POSITIONS

First, some notes about my terminology. In this book you will see words like women, feminist, privilege, Other, queer, 2SLGBTQIA+, Black, and so on that have contentious understandings. I define and bold them as they appear—as I did above with "body stories"—in order to give a sense of how I am using them and/or how they are used by various thinkers. I do this because it is crucially important for you to understand the depth and complexity of these words.

Secondly, I want to express something of my own positionality. I identify as an extremely tall, white, settler, cisgender, highly educated, privileged woman. I also identify as an **ally**. For me, this means that I aim to actively and consistently practise reflection on what I do or say as a person in a position of privilege and power in an attempt to work in solidarity with marginalized groups. In this book, I prioritize the body stories of the women I spoke with in order for their thoughts and experiences to shine through, so you will see longer-than-usual quotes from them. I know that voices of white feminists have far too often taken centre stage and made invisible the voices of marginalized women and non-binary folk. I do not want this to be further replicated here.

Lastly, as I noted earlier, I often talk directly to you. I know that this is not necessarily a common occurrence in a book such as this, but this is a book filled with conversations. Some of these conversations will make you feel like a spectator, and some will make you feel like an insider, but I hope all will engage you. We all live through our bodies in some way and, in that respect, there is an "us" that matters. We all have a body and a story that goes along with it.

THE BODY

The body is a complicated idea. We have a body and, to some extent, are our body. Our physical body is what keeps us alive, but our embodied experiences are what forms our relationships and adds significance to our lives. **Embodiment** usually refers to the relationship between the body and its interactive processes, such as perception through the senses, and how these interactions aid, enhance, or interfere with our social experiences. Embodiment is a process of meaning-making where our physical experiences, through bodily form, gaze, gesture, body posture, facial expression, and movement, shapes the form of our interactions with social and cultural environments. Embodiment can also be conceived of in representations of bodies, like avatars, which offer a form of "virtual" embodiment. Such environments offer new ways to "embody" a set of identities outside one's own physical being, where the virtual avatar acts as a tool through which identity can be shaped. It is through a discussion of embodiment that we can see how our bodies are the space and place of all the meaning that transpires in life, from our birth until our death.

A key theory to understanding how bodies are social creations is through **social constructionism**. If we look at the things in our lives, they themselves do not have meaning, but we construct meaning for these things using systems of representation, such as language. We name things. The name and the thing are not connected in any natural way, but it is through language that the way we represent things comes to be seen as natural. The key idea in this is "construct"; to construct something means to build or create it. The constructionist approach does not prioritize "things" as having natural qualities; rather, it explores how these qualities are taught, learned, and reproduced through social interactions and relations. In this way, we can define representation as the creation and production of the meanings that we give to things in our minds through the use of language. As an example, imagine a sign for a gendered public washroom and consider: What is the symbol representing? How do you know? What language could you use to describe the image you see in your mind? Now, imagine a non-gendered sign. What would that look like? How would you describe it?

In 2003, Susan Bordo, a prominent feminist thinker on the politics of women's bodies, wrote that the **body** is "a powerful symbolic form, a surface on which the central rules, hierarchies, and even metaphysical commitments of a culture are inscribed and thus reinforced through the concrete language of the body. The body may also operate as a metaphor for culture" (165). We can see this through the ways that body ideals for women have changed over time—if we examine Sandro Botticelli's *The Birth of Venus* (completed in 1486), it was hailed as the ultimate idealization of female beauty for generations. It depicts the goddess Venus arriving at the shore after her birth, when she had emerged from the sea fully grown. Her body resembles some of the markers of contemporary idealized femininity—fair skin, long body, long hair—but her body shape would be considered too large to be ideal by today's standards. Popular culture often dictates what form and shape our bodies should be for them to be **normal** and desirable (these are ideas we will return to in Chapter 2), but we now live in a time where most of the images of bodies that we see are filtered, altered, airbrushed, and shrunk, and have undergone so many manipulations that they can no longer be considered meaningful human representations.

"The body is not only a text of culture. It is also … a practical, direct locus of social control" (Bordo 2003, 165). Our bodies are made through our relations with one another; some call our bodies docile, meaning that they are almost submissive to the influence of the people, cultures, and communities that they coexist with. Our bodies exist within the boundaries of cultural structures, and it is not possible for us to separate them from our social lives. This is referring to how bodies exist within **power** relations, which is an idea we will continually return to. Michel Foucault (1990) sees power as ever-present, "because it is produced from one moment to the next, at every point, or rather in every relation from one point to another. Power is everywhere; not because it embraces everything, but because it comes from everywhere" (93). We often imagine that those at the top of the social hierarchy are the only ones with power—this is not accurate. Power is a more fluid concept than that. We can enact power in a variety of ways depending on our identities and the spaces we move through. While it is absolutely correct to say that hegemonic (meaning: dominant forms of) masculinity and whiteness prevail in society as privileged identities, this does not mean everyone else is completely disempowered. It does mean that we have to imagine power in other ways—this can be seen through our desires for social change, grassroots social movements, personal and political uprisings, and other forms of resistance and activism that we may partake in.

IDENTITY

We all have **identities**. Our identities make up who we are and how we understand and form relationships to one another. When we think of our identities, they are often in relation to other people—sibling, child, student, employee, partner—but they are also in specific relation to aspects of ourselves—our gender, race, sexuality, disability, age, religion, and ethnicity, to name just a few. When we start to unpack these identities, which for the purposes of this book will be primarily Western in focus, we come to recognize that the application and experience of these identities are complex. The identities that help to construct our bodies are complicated and dynamic for all of us. One of the ways that I approach understanding how power relations are connected to identities is through Judith Butler's explanation of how our identities come to be recognized. As Butler (2005) states, "[t]he norms by which I seek to make myself recognizable are not fully mine. They are not born with me; the temporality of their emergence does not coincide with the temporality of my own life" (35). Butler's framing of identities within terms of recognition positions them not as a trait that an individual possesses, but rather as contextually produced by way of the particular kinds of acts each of us perform and how we perform together.

When considering these identities, they need to be framed in terms of intersectionality. The term intersectionality was coined by Black feminist scholar Kimberlé Williams Crenshaw in 1989, and has since become pivotal in our understanding of identities. **Intersectionality** refers to the ways that our identities are never disconnected from each other. When we think about bodies and identities, we need to use an intersectional analytical approach. Intersectional analyses suggest that biological, social, and cultural categories such as gender, race, class, ability, sexual orientation, and other axes of identity interact and intersect on multiple and often simultaneous levels. These intersections lead some to experience social **privilege**, which positions certain bodies as having unearned advantages that are systemically created and culturally reinforced. Privileged bodies are those that are seen and legible as a body—those bodies welcomed for how they appear, behave, and exist in certain spaces and cultures. Not all bodies are equally visible, and some may not want to be seen at all. Interestingly, there are privileges of being visible and/or invisible, which exist because of the idea that there is a "normal body," which Chapter 2 will cover extensively.

These relational elements of identity also lead people to experience systemic inequality. Crenshaw articulated the ways in which Black women's experiences need to be discussed in greater complexity, a new idea at the time. She states:

> ... I am suggesting that Black women can experience discrimination in ways that are both similar to and different from those experienced by white women and Black men. Black women sometimes experience discrimination in ways similar to white women's experiences; sometimes they share very similar experiences with Black men. Yet often they experience double-discrimination—the combined effects of practices which discriminate on the basis of race, and on the basis of sex. And sometimes, they experience discrimination as Black women—not the sum of race and sex discrimination, but as Black women. (Crenshaw 1989, 149)

Crenshaw's positioning of the ways that power, identities, and oppressions are always working together and always intersecting has fostered the foundational way we understand inequities and the complexities of identities today. When I teach this concept, I tell my students that I can never be thought of as "just" a woman; rather, I am a white woman with significant social privilege. For example, while I have experienced sexism, I have experienced sexism through the lens of whiteness, and my whiteness must be understood as inextricable from my experience of gender (and all of my other identities as well).

Oppressions within society, such as racism, sexism, homophobia, etc., do not exist independently of one another; instead, these forms of oppression interrelate, creating a system of oppression that reflects the "intersection" of multiple forms of discrimination. We must always consider that these interactions are never external to notions of power.

More specifically, intersectional analyses suggest that biological, social, and cultural categories such as gender, race, class, ability, sexual orientation, and other axes of identity interact and intersect on multiple and often simultaneous levels.

GENDER

Gender is a foundational idea in culture and the major undercurrent connecting the participants in this book. It is not a biological identity, but rather a social one. Gender refers to the socially constructed roles, behaviours, activities, and attributes that relate to understandings of masculinity, femininity, and non-binary attributes in any given society. Drawing from the social sciences' symbolic interactionist tradition, we can think of gender as more of a verb than a noun or an adjective—we all *do* gender, embedding it in the way we relate to other people. It is much better to think of gender as a *process*. This perspective on gender focuses on everyday life and how people communicate with and act toward each other. If you consider what you do to prepare your body for the day, there are choices that you are expected to make. Clothes. Hair. Makeup (or no makeup). Jewellery. These choices carry markers of gender with them. Some people use them to fulfill gendered expectations; some people use them to resist gendered expectations. Either way, we live in a world where gender is always a process and an expectation.

In most societies, gender has historically been organized hierarchically. Quite often, one gender is associated with holding privilege and power in most domains of life, such as the ability to lead a country as an elected official, while the other only takes up these privileges as an exception rather than the rule. In Western societies at least, gender is also frequently understood as a power dynamic within a binary; if one is masculine, one cannot by definition also take on the attributes of femininity as it is framed as *less than*. In other words, value and status may be afforded to one gender more than the other, and these advantages are sometimes gained at the expense of the other. As you already know, this book focuses on the experiences of **women**, and my use of that term is an inclusive one. I define a woman to be a person who identifies as a woman; this can include **cisgender** women (preferring to remain in the gender assigned at birth), **transgender** women (those who move away from the gender assigned at birth), femme/feminine-identifying genderqueer people, and non-binary folks. Beyond this, the categories through which people can identify in terms of their gender are ever expanding, including agender, genderless, and genderfluid, and certainly in other ways that have yet to be commonly defined. These ideas will be further elaborated on in Chapter 3.

Much work has been done to recognize the limitations imposed by gendered hierarchies and binaries. Despite the existence of rules about gender, most of us can think of multiple examples where those rules are contradicted, including within our own experiences. As a social product, gender is manifested in the ways that people interact with each other. Defining gender strictly in terms of a singular masculinity or femininity is problematic as it implies that only two separate and discrete gender categories exist. So, instead of saying masculinity or femininity, it is important to pluralize these terms—masculinities and femininities. One aspect of the complexity of gender talk stems from the ways that understandings of gender are understood to be natural: "Gender difference ... is largely culturally constructed, yet appears entirely natural" (DeMello 2014, 118). It is the appearance of naturalness that makes the discussion of gender so frustrating at times because it feels instinctual to us, when it is entirely learned behaviour. When we discuss gender, we need to think about how it is constructed "through exclusionary means, such that the human is not only produced over and against the inhuman, but through a set of foreclosures, radical erasures, that are, strictly speaking, refused the possibility of cultural articulation" (Butler 1993, 8). As Butler explains, to be slotted into the subject position of the normal human—and in her example here she is referring to the masculine—is one of extreme power in that the focus of all major social institutions and socializing/educating practices becomes interrelated with reinforcing what is ideal—the normal, masculine human.

RACE

Race, like gender, is both an identity and a social institution, because these are social constructions that we use to make sense of ourselves and categories through which societies are organized. The physical differences that many people think of as "race" mean very little biologically. However, they mean a great deal culturally and socially. "Race is a social, economic, and political system of division and inequality" (DeMello 2014, 101). Inherited traits such as the colour of one's skin or the texture of one's hair have, throughout modern history, become associated with the concept of race. Skin colour and hair texture are no different from other inherited physical traits—such as height or eye colour—and they are far more difficult to distinguish with precision, but throughout modern history, these traits have been given arbitrary significance, often in the service of defining membership to a ruling class versus people whose labour could be exploited. Vic Satzewich and Nikolaos Liodakis (2013) argue that "race" (which they consistently place in quotation marks to indicate that it is a constructed term) has come to have meaning over time through pseudo-scientific classifications, which were used to foster "biologically informed racism" (14). The authors argue that while this was a historical occurrence, racially informed scientific practices continue today in order to attempt to prove that there are significant genetic differences between people of differing racial "origins." Again, these are relations of power. The power to relegate certain bodies as less or Other to privileged bodies (read: white bodies). You will notice that Other, in this instance, is spelled with a capital "O." This is to mark the difference between other people—in whatever way they may be similar to yourself—and Other people—those who experience some form of social marginalization that you do not.

Perhaps a better way to think about these constructions of gender and race is that we, collectively, create them. The limits of language, Satzewich and Liodakis (2013) point out, mean that we use the term "race" to mean a wide variety of things and "despite the analytical problems with the concept of 'race,' Canadian society still tries to measure and quantify 'race' and 'racial diversity'" (20). The relevance of "race" is further evidenced by the ways that racial identity is managed through the manipulation of laws, politics, citizenship, and the distribution of resources. News media, for example, are frequently complicit in reinforcing biological notions of "race" as unchanging and fixed, particularly in terms of a supposed dangerous Other, thereby shaping public notions of who is a "real" Canadian and who is understood as an outsider. These ideas are colonial in origin.

Colonization is a lived and ongoing reality in Canada. According to Sheila Cote-Meek (2014), "[c]olonization is conceptualized as having four dimensions—it concerns the land, it requires a specific structure of ideology to proceed, it is violent, and it is ongoing" (18). These realities of colonization are complex and speak to how the colonizers' desire for land has led to the dehumanization of Indigenous peoples; violent, forced assimilation; cultural genocide; and the ongoing racist and exclusionary practices that Indigenous peoples have experienced in Canada for generations. The use of the word Indigenous to describe Indigenous peoples is a choice. As Linda Tuhiwai Smith (2012) notes,

> "Indigenous peoples" is a relatively recent term which emerged in the 1970s out of the struggles primarily of the American Indian Movement (AIM), and the Canadian Indian Brotherhood. It is a term that internationalizes the experiences, the issues and the struggles of some of the world's colonized peoples. The final "s" in "peoples" has been argued for quite vigorously by [I]ndigenous activists because of the right of peoples to self-determination. It is also used as a way of recognizing that there are real differences between different [I]ndigenous peoples. (7)

Tuhiwai Smith (2012) is speaking to the importance of naming practices and notably asserts that "Indigenous" can also be problematic as it "appears to collectivize many distinct populations whose experiences under imperialism have been vastly different" (6). I have chosen to use "Indigenous peoples" and perspectives in this book in order to speak to the most inclusive usage of the term in Canada, while recognizing its potential exclusions. If our aim is to foster inclusive dialogue, then privileging Indigenous perspectives "involves understanding that being *Indigenous* and being *woman* are derived from the relationships established with place, spiritual beings, humans, and the environment" (Altamirano-Jiménez and Kermoal 2016, 9). Again, it is important to note the limits of language and reflect on this reality through all discussions of bodies and identities.

Above, I have used words such as "normal" and "real" in quotation marks to indicate that these are contested ideas. Whiteness is undeniably the privileged race across the world, and it is very important to name it that way. White bodies are often considered to be "unmarked" bodies. In Richard Dyer's (1997) *White*, he claims that "[a] person is deemed visibly white because of a quite complicated interaction of elements, of which flesh tones within the pink to beige range are only one: the shape of the nose, eyes and lips, the colour and set of hair, even body shape may all be mobilized to determine someone's 'colour'" (42). These constructions serve to support the racist notion that whiteness offers "the prestige of being better and superior; it is the promise of being more human, more full, less lacking" (Seshandri-Crooks 2000, 7). Furthering this idea, Ruth Frankenberg and Peggy McIntosh are often credited as creators of a body of feminist theory that has sought to form an ongoing account of the social, political, and cultural advantages afforded to white people in Western society. In particular, Frankenberg's study of white women enables thinking through whiteness as a site for both the reproduction of racism and for challenges to it. Frankenberg (1993) claims that whiteness must be understood to be similar to how masculinity is gendered—these aspects of identity are socially constructed and yet have real privileged effects that must be seen as "interconnected" with other aspects of identity.

Similarly, in McIntosh's (1990) often-cited piece "White Privilege: Unpacking the Invisible Knapsack," she argues that "whites are taught to think of their lives as morally neutral, normative, and average, and also ideal" (32–33). She infers that white people receive social advantages that are conveyed through these notions of neutrality and this neutrality renders the advantages invisible to most white people, but visible to marginalized Others. She also provides a thoughtful warning: "Since racism, sexism, and heterosexism are not the same, the advantages associated with them should not be seen as the same" (McIntosh 1990, 35). While McIntosh doesn't use the language of intersectionality, you can see it underpinning the previous quote.

DISABILITY

Disability is an identity that is also integral to consider when we are discussing the ways that bodies appear. **Disability**, much like gender and race, can be defined as a representation, a cultural interpretation of bodily difference, and a comparison of bodies that structures social relations and institutions. Scholars in feminist disability studies often explore how bodies labelled as "abnormal" appear in social space, in order to deconstruct how bodies are constructed to represent social ills or deviance. Disability scholars and activists argue that it is in fact the world that is built improperly for some bodies and the problems never lie in disabled bodies, but in disabling environments (Fritsch 2019). In relation to disabled bodies, Rosemarie Garland-Thomson contends that "abnormal" bodies are stareable because they contradict the normalcy that we have come to expect from everybody: "The site of an unexpected body—that is to say, a body that does not conform to our expectations for an ordinary body—is compelling because it disorders expectations. Such disorder is at once novel and disturbing" (Garland-Thomson 2009, 37). From infancy, bodies are disciplined in attempts to make them seem as normal as possible through our appearance, and behaviours and failing to seem "normal" has social consequences.

Thinking about disability as socially constructed differs from the more common approach to studying disability—as something that needs to be repaired because it is wrong. **Ability** is a signifier for normalcy—whatever normalcy is in a particular cultural moment, space, or time defines what ability is. The disabled body/identity acts as a social signifier for deviancy (the abnormal). "Because disability is defined not as a set of observable, predictable traits—like racialized or gendered features—but rather any departure from an unstated physical or functional norm, disability highlights individual differences. In other words, the concept of disability unites a highly marked, heterogeneous group whose only commonality is being considered abnormal" (Garland-Thomson 1997, 24). It is through this loose definition that it becomes clear that disability is socially constructed. The constructed nature of disability is characterized by such factors as: expectations of performance; the pace of life; the physical and social organization of social environments to fit a young, nondisabled, "ideally" shaped, healthy adult (male) citizen; cultural representations; failure of representations; visible/invisible representations; and discrimination. The defining of certain bodies as problems, as wrong, and as bad is the oppression that is at the core of the disability rights movement: "Locating the problems of social injustice in the world, rather than in our bodies, has been key to naming oppression" (Clare 2001, 360). It is also important to acknowledge that, when I state above that disability is an identity that is also integral to consider when we are discussing the ways that bodies appear, I am also being exclusionary in my discussion of bodies. I am privileging the dominant understanding of the world as one where people use vision to see and read one another. I recognize that this is a limited stance to take. While the visual is an element of how people initially interact with one another, it is not the only sense we rely on—we communicate through language, touch, smell, and feelings. The visual is a major element of this project, but it is not the only one.

THEORIES OF APPEARING AND STARING

The ideas of bodies and identity that I have introduced are deeply rooted in feminist thinking. I recognize that the word **feminism** can be contentious, as it is variously represented and misrepresented both historically and contemporarily. As the MeToo and TimesUp movements have been gaining traction in the last few years, the language of feminism has become much more salient in society as of late. I believe that beginning from a basic understanding of feminism is always the best course of action: "Feminism is a movement to end sexism, sexist exploitation, and oppression" (hooks 2000, viii). It is the belief and the framework through which we can understand that all genders are equal and they should be treated as such. Feminist ideas and theoretical frameworks focus on embracing the complexity of our identities and uncovering relations of power that serve to disadvantage and marginalize people (such as sexism and racism), while understanding that discriminations should not be made based on differences in biology, gender, sexuality, race, culture, age, disability, religion, or appearance.

From childhood, "human beings are trained to visually process and meticulously read bodies—our own and others—for social cues about love, beauty, status, and identity" (Casper and Moore 2009, 1). As social beings, "[w]e relish looking, produce endless images, and root our understanding of the world in observation. Indeed, most information comes to us through sight in this intensely technological world saturated with advertising and crowded with computer, television, and video screens" (Garland-Thomson 2009, 25). Similarly, Tanya Titchkosky (2007) claims that the process of appearing is an active and engaged process: "People enact appearance and thereby make something appear, not as just sheer arbitrary stuff, but as meaningful stuff. We can, and often must, act as if something 'has' meaning in itself" (23). We are taught to covet the familiar and to question the unusual. What these terms can mean vary from person to person, of course. But if we look to popular media as a key site of where we learn what bodies are supposed to look like—particularly women's bodies—the range of what is considered normal (and subsequently good) is quite narrow. White, thin, young, able-bodied, not too tall nor short, and readably feminine are the general markers of a normal woman's body in Canadian society.

This is where the **public scrutiny** of our bodies comes in. Public scrutiny is when a person or thing is being watched, observed, and assessed—very carefully—by other people. Through the element of assessment, this scrutiny can morph into interactions, such as pointing, laughing, questioning, and commenting. John Berger (1972) once said that "[t]o look is an act of choice" (8). Similarly, to allow our looks to linger is also a choice because to stare at something or someone is to form a connection to it. When and how our bodies appear to other people matters to us. We have mirrors for a reason. We want to see how we look, decide if that look is great, good, passible, or shameful. We hate stares, and we desire and yearn for stares. We want them for some reasons, but not for others. Garland-Thomson wrote a formative book in 2009 called *Staring: How We Look*. She has greatly influenced my thinking on how staring forces an encounter between a starer and a staree, and I return to her insights throughout the course of this book.

A staring encounter has consequences—in terms of communication, meaning-making, and the emotions it fosters. The basis for a stare is fairly simple. Garland-Thomson (2009) states: "We stare when ordinary seeing fails, when we want to know more. So staring is an interrogative gesture that asks what's going on and demands the story. The eyes hang on, working to recognize what seems illegible, order what seems unruly, know what seems strange" (3). Our world is highly organized through the visual—we depend on sight as the primary sensory conduit that structures our being in the world.

The ways that we process the variations between our bodies is rarely neutral. We ascribe meanings onto the differences we perceive—regardless of how physiologically or culturally minor they should be—and we then give those differences intense social significance. We stare at each other to try to make sense of the unexpected, but, as I said above, there are consequences to staring and to being stared at. "Because we come to expect one another to have certain kinds of bodies and behaviors, stares flare up when we glimpse people who look or act in ways that contradict our expectations. Seeing startlingly stareable people challenges our assumptions by interrupting complacent visual business-as-usual" (Garland-Thomson 2009, 6). This is the reason for staring, but for those who have unusual bodies being stared at can illicit many feelings—embarrassment, fear, annoyance, anger, and so on. Many people could say that these responses are overreactions, but as you will see throughout this book, our body stories are often built upon lifelong staring interactions. Stares lead to comments, questions, gestures, dialogue, and sometimes violence for those with non-conforming embodiments.

It is through these interactions that we can see how our experiences in public settings are unique and based on a wide array of intersectional factors. You might be able to relate and recall experiences where strangers asked you a question about your appearance that caught you off guard and made you question how you look to them and others. My intention in having you consider this is in order to emphasize how our place in public spaces is inherently political. To say that some element of life is political refers to how every culture and community has a different perspective on who gets to decide and enforce the way practices and beliefs are enacted—this can refer to the power of our governance on a large or small scale. When we discuss place, it can be defined as a physical setting in which our experiences occur. This is referring to all of the geographical locations of our lives—global, national, local, virtual. Space, on the other hand, is usually framed as more abstract and subjective (Gieseking and Mangold, 2014). Space is how we give places meaning—our experiences, achievements, values, representations, and feelings that we give to places. Our engagements in public space can be fraught with exhilaration, awe, pain, shame, and fear through our engagements with others in these spaces. These emotive moments of our lives help to dictate the relationships that we form with ourselves and other people.

THE ROLE OF INTERPRETATION

Interpretation is a key element of the role of appearing and looking. As I noted above, the structure of this book is based on my interest in combining body stories with theory and artistic interpretation. I wanted to include this rather unusual element because I think that it is important to recognize our ways of seeing: "Yet, although every image embodies a way of seeing, our perception or appreciation of an image depends also upon our own way of seeing" (Berger 1972, 10). When you read the body stories of each participant, you will construct your own vision of what they may look like and we will present you with Damian's visual interpretation.

As a graphic designer, Damian's approach to this project was to cast his plans aside. Damian says,

> When I started this project, I had this wonderful process in place and I had also a predicted look and style that I was going for. As a

visual artist, most of the illustrations that I make are self-created and self-processed. For this project, the moment I started to read through the transcripts, I knew my process was going to be tossed out the window. I had to be fully open to the emotional experiences that all these women went through. My process moved from quickly trying to sum up what I thought these women looked like and trying to craft that to crying, laughing, and getting really fucking pissed off on their behalf. Who these women are and everything about them, including the way they talked and the way they answered questions about themselves and their experiences, just got thrown into the sky almost like a Jell-O salad. I was left trying to gather moments and ideas that I felt best represented the most powerful, authentic representation of who these amazing women are.

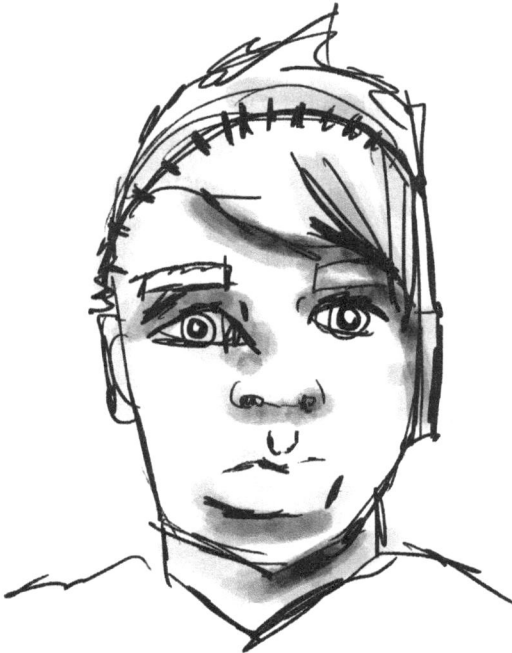

Figure 1.1. Self-portrait
Damian Mellin, 2020

Damian's identities are integral to how this project has unfolded. He acknowledges that he comes from a great deal of privilege: "I'm tall and white with straight blond hair, blue eyes." He also recognizes that how we look does not reflect the depth of our experiences.

> Much like the participants in this book, I am not what I may appear to be. For most of my life, I have been hiding the inner pages. The fear of being caught has caused an overwhelming panic that has forced me to the brink of suicide. As someone who has extreme learning disabilities, I always fear that my career and work is in jeopardy. As someone who is always dancing on the gender spectrum, I have tried to play the role of the guy's guy. As a queer artist, I have felt like my private life has often been at odds with my professional life. I have recently come out to people in my life about my debilitating depression. Taking people at face value—whatever that is—is no longer possible.

As you will see, this book intermingles feminist and sociological theory, personal narrative from interviews, and commissioned drawings strictly based on the body stories of participants. These stories are unique and would change if I spoke with the participants today. These stories are also not all-encompassing. There are many elements of bodies not covered in these pages as it is not possible to incorporate body stories here beyond those that were shared with me. For example, none of the participants identify as disabled, but discussions of disability proliferate as disability studies and relations to disability from many of the participants are relevant. It is through these relations that intersectional approaches to the body can be best understood. Body stories are never complete, never the same, never finished.

THE BODY STORIES

As I said earlier, there are eight body stories in this book: Nana, Rae, Kali, Alice, Gioia, Viola, Quinn, and my own story. The first seven names are all pseudonyms that the participants have chosen for themselves in order to protect their anonymity. I found these seven women through a call for participants on Twitter and Facebook. The call read:

Victoria Kannen
@victoriakannen

Writing a book on bodies & public space in Canada. Looking to interview women & non-binary folks who have experience with comments, stares, questions, etc. from strangers bc of your odd/awe-inspiring body. Send me a DM! Please RT. #storytelling #bodies #feminist @WomensPressCA

6:52 PM · Jan 6, 2020 · Twitter for iPhone

Figure 1.2. Tweet 1
Twitter: @victoriakannen, 2020

Of those who contacted me, I chose to interview the people who I felt had the most to say about their embodied experiences and seemed most eager to share their story. I asked to interview women and non-binary folks because of how systemic discrimination, along with the historical connections that tie femininities and non-normative gender presentations to being less-than, position these bodies as always already publicly available for comment, critique, and inquiry.

This book uses qualitative methodology. Specifically, I have used two forms of qualitative methods to create this project. The primary practice involves using semi-structured audio-recorded interviews, because the use of interviews allows me to explore the participants' perceptions in a manner that can most effectively illustrate how they consider their body and their interactions surrounding it, how they self-identify, and so on. I see the role of storytelling in this way to be a feminist practice as I create space for folks to share their story, use their own words, and base my writing—in coordination with their ideas—on their lived experience. In my work, I strive to prioritize the lives and stories of women and non-binary people.

The strategy to include personal narratives (a.k.a. the body stories) is important for a number of reasons. First, these subjective expressions are the moments that allow you to connect with examples that come from diverse perspectives. If the voice of this book was mostly my own, without other narratives of embodiment, then the privilege that I experience as a white, tall, thin, able-bodied woman is overshadowing the plethora of voices that can speak to how embodiments exist in odd and awe-some ways. Second, this is an element of accessible learning. The inclusion of conversations is important because it somewhat breaks from more traditional theory, which can be intimidating to students and those readers outside of academia. The aim was to talk to people who are not strictly scholars—which is an exclusivity that sometimes happens in academic publishing— but rather people who feel that their bodies are the subject of awe and oddity. Third, creating new research on the subject of bodies is vital. When teaching courses on bodies and embodiment, it is often difficult to find texts that politicize bodies without being too geared to one element of identity—such as gender or race—or texts generally focus on embodied extremes, such as radical body modification. Presenting body stories using an intersectional approach enables aspects of identity and body modifications to be discussed, but they are balanced between the everyday experiences of public interactions and odd (rather than extreme) embodiments. The body stories devoted to them are just an introduction to who they are and what we discussed. In each theory chapter, the details of their body stories will be expressed and theorized in more detail.

The interviews took place in person with those who lived close enough to meet and over the phone for the rest. All interviews were recorded and conducted in January and February 2020, immediately prior to the COVID-19 pandemic. Each participant signed an informed consent document, and we agreed that their identities would be kept anonymous.

The second qualitative method is an artist's interpretation through representation. This was the call that I released in order to connect with an artist:

Victoria Kannen
@victoriakannen

I am looking to commission an artist to create 6 or 7 portraits of women & non-binary folks for an upcoming book (as well as creating the cover image). My DMs are open if you would like more info! Please share/RT. #art #pedagogy #feminism #bodypolitics #publishing @WomensPressCA

10:29 AM · Oct 21, 2019 · Twitter for iPhone

Figure 1.3. Tweet 2
Twitter: @victoriakannen, 2020

It was important to me that I work with someone who was political in their work and who was highly interested in collaborating on this project, specifically. I wanted to work with an artist who was open to a non-conventional approach: creating art based strictly on their interpretations of the transcripts of our interviews, not actually seeing or hearing any of the participants. Luckily, Damian was one of the artists who responded to the call and we connected immediately.

As discussed above, Damian explores how he threw his original ideas away once he began working on the art, but I believe it is important to read his statement:

The stories and self-expression that you will read in this book are from women speaking their whole truths—the non-glossy, non-Instagrammable truths of living in a world where women face many varied experiences. I am just the man who has had the luxury of illustrating them. It is truly my recommendation that you stop reading my introduction. If you still wish to push ahead with my words, I will tell you why I think this book is very important. So often, we make very quick assumptions about who people are and how they can benefit us. Our instant evaluation skills are composed of what our family upbringing has taught us, what society has shown us and the laziness of our brains in a world overwhelmed by mundane details that have very little value. Who we are is not something that can be summed up in a second, or a page, or a book. The uniqueness of each person and their stored potential has the power to reshape us all. You not only owe it to the people around you, but you also really owe it to yourself to give space for people to share uniqueness.

Within the process of illustrating the participants, I wanted to take a medium that historically gave women very little depth: a vintage comic book style. The comic books of the 1950s to the 1970s offered very little imagination of who women were outside of their trophy, idealized status. The idea of turning that style against the oppression that those comic books created tickled my interest. As a comic book reader in the 1990s and onward—where women were fully fleshed out characters like Storm, Wonder Woman, and Catwoman—the idea of showcasing these women as super and brave made a lot of sense. Although each illustration turned the idea of comic books on its head, each illustration took something from their story and reimagined them as the hero of their own story.

The illustrations of each body story will appear after my introduction of each participant and before the chapter where they are discussed. Below every illustration, Damian's explanation will appear. I wanted you to hear how and why he created them in the ways that he did, what he saw when he read their words, and what he imagined them to look like. To me, the art gives some coherence to the body stories; it allows you to imagine them, to foster your own ideas, which may or may not align with Damian's, and to consider what it means to have an image of someone based on words alone.

BOOK SECTIONS

Normally, a fairly detailed summary of each chapter would appear here, but I often find this convention a bit redundant. Instead, I will provide a brief description of the major chapters.

Chapter 2—Well-Meaning Strangers: Identities, Stares, and Hair

This chapter is based on Nana and Rae's body stories. Theories are discussed that further elaborate on the complexity of identities, the social politics of staring in public, and the ways in which hair manifests as gendered and racialized signifiers. A key contribution of this chapter is the concept of "the well-meaning stranger" and the ways that interactions in public—even when they are coming from good intentions—can have long-lasting consequences in terms of how scrutiny can impact people's perceptions of themselves.

Chapter 3—Our Bodies as Private and Public (Sexualized) Spaces

This chapter is based on Kali and Alice's body stories. This chapter focuses on sexuality, sexualization, the role of space and place, fetishization, and exoticism. The concept of power is discussed in depth in order to explore key concepts such as heteronormativity, homonormativity, and patriarchy.

Chapter 4—Underestimated and Overdetermined: Shame, Tokenism, Exoticism, and Fierce Resistance

This chapter is based on Viola and Gioia's body stories. The focus of Chapter 4 is to explore in-between experiences of Indigeneity, passing, and tokenism. The role of shame and various understandings of resistance—in terms of race, body size, and what it can mean to be "fierce"—is key to understanding Viola and Gioia's stories, so these concepts are explored in significant depth as well.

Chapter 5—Excessive Bodies: Modified and (Un)Natural Freaks

This chapter is based on the body stories of Quinn and myself. Theories in this chapter focus on histories of embodied difference via the freak show and how those historical markers persist. This chapter explores disability, height, and body modifications. As this chapter features my body story, it does take on a more personal tone, while it also incorporates some additional connections to Kali and Alice's stories.

Chapter 6—Bodies and Their Stories

This is the concluding chapter of the book. While it discusses possibilities for future research, it also explores the role of pedagogy as it relates to bodies and body stories. After hearing some concluding thoughts from the participants, the chapter ends by encouraging personal reflection through stories and art.

At the end of each chapter, you will notice that there is a Key Words section. The words that appear in this section have been bolded in the chapter and defined in order for your reading to be as accessible as possible. These words are also explained again in the Glossary. Following the Key Words section in each chapter, there are Questions for Reflection and Discussion. I hope that these help to frame your response to the chapters and help you to further engage with the ideas you have just read.

After Chapter 6, you will find the Appendix. In this Appendix, there are more Questions for Reflection and Discussion that have been created in order to extend your engagement with the stories, art, and concepts once you complete the book. References are the last section of the book.

KEY WORDS

Ability; Ally; Body; Body stories; Cisgender; Colonization; Disability; Embodiment; Feminism; Gender; Identities; Intersectionality; Normal; Oppression; Power; Privilege; Public scrutiny; Race; Social constructionism; Transgender; Women

QUESTIONS FOR REFLECTION AND DISCUSSION

1. What are some of the ways that your body has been commented on by a stranger? Why do you think you remember that encounter?

2. Why are so many conversations about gender connected to the experiences of women? Why do you think that no self-identified men responded to the call for this book?
3. Think about this sentence: "We all have a body and, to some extent, are our bodies." If you were to explain this sentence in your own words, what would you say?

CHAPTER 2

Well-Meaning Strangers: Identities, Stares, and Hair

Body Story: Nana

I'm so grateful for this experience. I think it's really important to talk about the co-created nature of perception. We do it together.

—Nana

Nana identifies herself as a white, settler, cis, queer, 30-year-old woman who is a mental health therapist living in Southern Ontario. Our conversation was winding and reflexive. We talked about disability, queerness, pop culture, neoliberalism, whiteness, shame, and love. I decided to start with her narrative because Nana was incredibly prepared to share her body story within our first few moments of chatting. She has experienced labels and diagnoses for body focused repetitive behaviours (BFRB); as she says, "I compulsively pull my hair out." She goes on to explain what this means in society and what this means for her:

Nana: BFRB is the umbrella term for this set of diagnosed mental illnesses or mental health issues. Compulsive hair-pulling also lives by the name trichotillomania, but it's now more formally referred to as compulsive hair-pulling. There's also dermatillomania, which is compulsive skin-picking. And that's a bit of my life too. It's the skin-picking and the hair-pulling that are my two pals ... and that's just the way that I am ... it is not a mental illness.

For those of you who are new to these discussions, this could be an off-putting presentation of one's self, but it is her confidence in who she is that makes Nana's narrative so compelling. Nana's claim to not having a mental illness is a political one, which she explains by stating:

Nana: I'm not distressed by my hair-pulling and I don't believe that I experience any impairments from it, so I decided that I actually don't have trichotillomania even though I compulsively pull my hair out. That is not a popular choice, but the label disempowered me. I reject it. But I don't talk about that a lot because folks kind of see me and see the way I look and seem to feel that it would be nice for me to have a diagnosis and simply say that I have this thing called trichotillomania and it means I pull my hair out. Actually, though, I don't. I prefer to sit a little bit more in the discomfort.

What it means for Nana to sit in the discomfort comes through in many forms. She told stories of initially hiding her bald patches, wig-wearing to conceal her hair-pulling, and her path to coming out as a bald queer femme woman. Her relationship to her now-shaved head and the assumptions that others share with her about it relate to concepts of visibility, invisibility, shame, and empowerment. As she says, "I feel really surveilled ... but my shaved head is precious to me. It keeps me well."

In our discussion, she explores the role of hair and hair-pulling in her life and the questions and assumptions that visible baldness brings with it. As you will see in this chapter, Nana has many stories of her encounters with what she calls "The Well-Meaning Stranger."

While our conversation was loaded with theory and challenging topics of discussion, we also talked about how her friends would describe her as having a strong duality: being both very serious and intense, while also being silly and irreverent. She thinks Natalie Portman, Kristen Stewart, or Florence Pugh would play her in a movie about her life. And that, very appropriately, if she were a cartoon character, she would be Nana from *Nanalan'*.

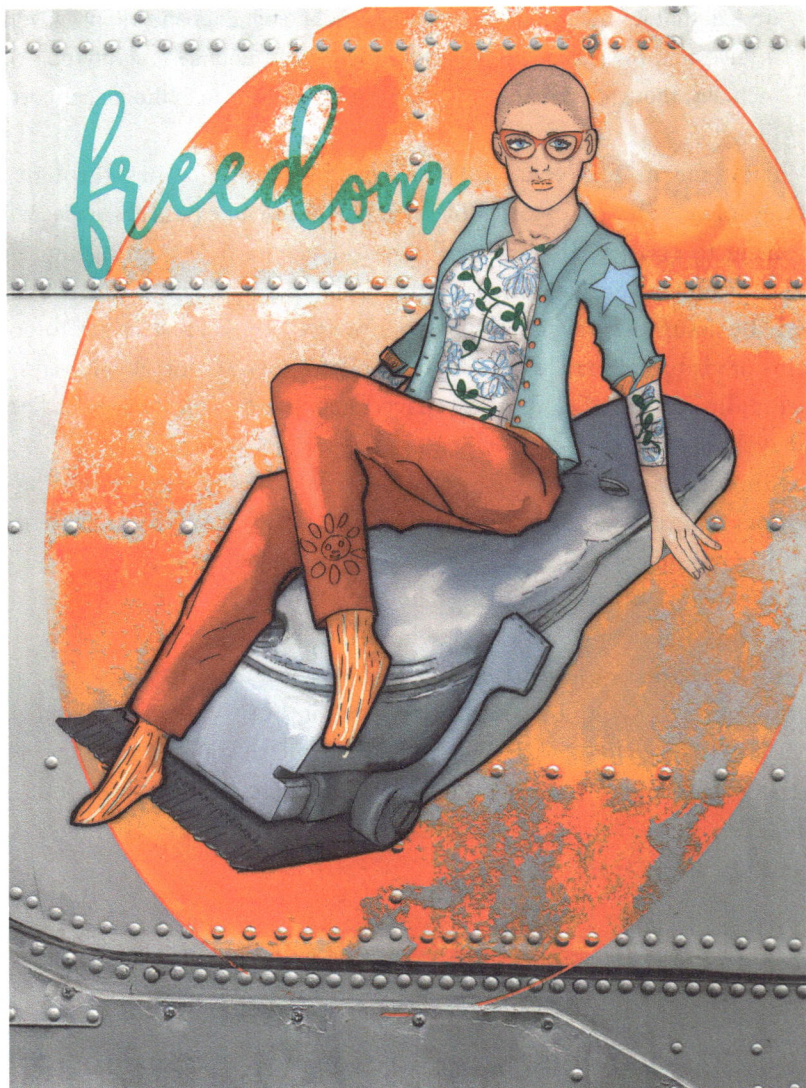

Nana
Damian Mellin, 2020

I really had no clue what I was going to do for Nana's piece. It wasn't until she communicated how shaving her head was a form of freedom that I began to have the image in my mind. I wanted to redefine what beauty is and when the words freedom and beauty are put together, I instantly think of the logos on World War II fighter planes. Nana riding her electric razor is a symbol I can get behind any day.—Damian Mellin

Body Story: Rae

You can't control other people's perceptions or the fact that they're going to throw assumptions onto you to try to "get you."
   —Rae

Rae is a 29-year-old Black woman living in a predominantly white, rural city in Ontario. She describes herself as being the "perfect height"—5 feet, 3 inches—and as a designer, her fashion sense is practical, but stylish. She embraces colour, dresses for comfort first, but loves a jumpsuit or pants on the usual. In describing her appearance, she says that there is always an accessory or statement piece that accentuates the feeling or look she wants her body to convey: "I don't think I'm super girly-girly, or dressing very feminine, but I do think that the silhouettes that I choose are similar types of colours or there's always an accessory that, while mostly not super feminine, I love a scarf or a head tie or a pair of earrings that add a little bit of a flourish." While she doesn't really wear make-up, when she does, she wants to "blow everyone out of the water" with how great she looks. In her answer to which five words she would use to describe herself, she didn't hesitate to say "thoughtful, curious, introverted, caring, and organized."

   Rae previously lived in Toronto, the UK, and the Caribbean, but she is Canadian. The places she has lived have dramatically impacted her understandings of self and the way that she presents in society. Regarding the city she currently lives in, she says, "This city is very, very white. Quite often I am the only Black person and the only person of colour in the room." Her body story tended to focus on two things: the way that people position her as Other, and the ways that people try to diminish her experience of being treated as Other. When explaining these experiences of racism, she feels this is the scenario that she most often deals with:

Someone: I think you are overreacting. Do you think you feel this way because you are looking to complain or whatever?

Rae: No, I'm pretty sure that because I have this unique experience that it means that I am good at identifying when it [racism] is happening. Not that I am paranoid or walking into a situation looking for or expecting it.

She says that people assume Canadian society is anti-racist; in comparison to the United States and their specific history of slavery, many Canadians respond with "at least we're not like that." Rae feels that even though she doesn't experience hate on an everyday basis, the accumulation of stares, questions, comments, touching (which we will discuss further in this chapter), and assumptions becomes tiresome.

Rae: It's like, I can't fit. There's only so much that I can control, right? And it is related to every part of who I am. I can't be like "Oh, I'm just not gonna be Black today," right? If something happens in the US and a Black person gets shot, I can't escape that reality. It is connected to my reality. I have no control over it.

Our topics of conversation were not always so heavy. In fact, much of my conversation with Rae was lighthearted and joyful. We talked about pop culture, boyfriends, "bonus" children, and food. At one point, I asked Rae what her favourite part of her body is. Her answer?

Rae: Oh, I love my eyes. The shape of my eyes. I think I have really nice eyelashes and they are not super long, but they're very curly. I never understood the eyelash curler things—which was another check your privilege moment where I just couldn't understand why people are using eyelash curlers! Then I realized, Oh, it's because they have straight eyelashes and they are out and everywhere! But yeah, I love my eyes.

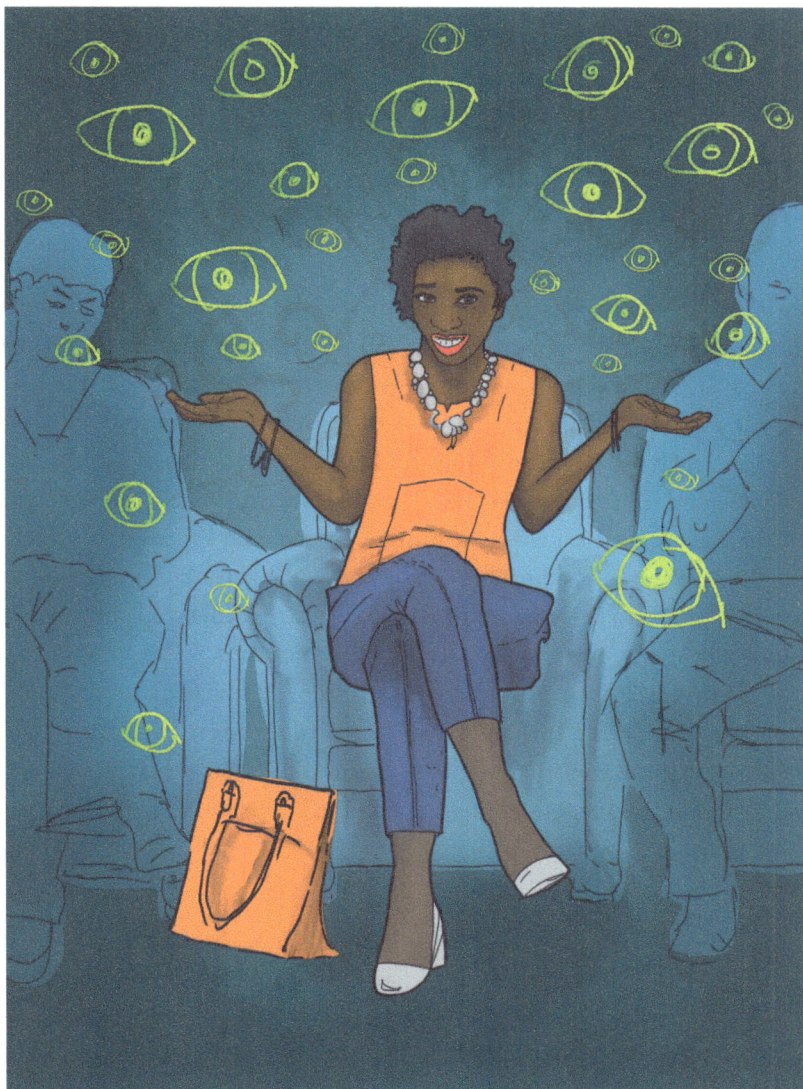

Rae
Damian Mellin, 2020

Can I say how much I love Rae? Is that allowed? Rae is the person in this book I would love to be the most like. She has the power to walk into any space and ignore the glaring eyes of hate. The inspiration for this piece is taken from cheesy 1990s movie posters. Now, we have Rae's movie: "Get out of my way. Have you seen my killer CV?"—Damian Mellin

Body Theories: Responding to Nana and Rae

IDENTITIES, STARES, AND ... HAIR?

Nana and Rae's body stories inspired the foundations of this chapter. Their experiences foster important introductions to the ways we identify ourselves and our engagements with other people. This chapter will begin by exploring theories of identities, such as gender and race, how identities shift as we age, and further shift based on where you are physically located. In my discussion with Nana, she introduced the concept of a "well-meaning stranger"—the kind of person who approaches someone they believe has an odd or awe-some body and has a comment or question that seems to be coming from a "good place." This well-meaning encounter, however, has consequences and, sometimes, those consequences lead to awkward or invasive questions, and even touching of a stranger's hair, as in Rae's case. The chapter will then turn to a more applied understanding of these concepts—relating back to the role of stares, strangers, and elements of our gendered and racialized appearances, such as hair.

IDENTITIES

Our bodies are not blank surfaces; they have recognizable features, forms, and styles that convey stories about them to other people. These stories are only partial tellings, of course, which is why many people approach bodies that are less recognizable in order to know more about them. The role of identity is foundational to understanding how bodies appear. Stuart Hall defines identity as an element of ourselves that can be seen as the meeting place between the individual and unique ways that we live our lives and the larger social discourses that position us. He says,

> I use identity to refer to the meeting point, the point of suture, between, on the one hand, the discourses and practices which attempt

to "interpellate," speak to us or hail us into place as the social subjects of particular discourses, and on the other hand, the processes that produce subjectivities, which construct us as subjects which can be "spoken." Identities are thus points of temporary attachment to the subject positions which discursive practices construct for us. (Hall 1996, 5–6)

Hall is saying that the social world that we are a part of connects with us and our identities through a process. This process is how society attempts to "interpellate" or give an identity to us in order to attempt to create who we are. However, these are not static elements of ourselves; rather, the meanings are always fluid. For example, our age changes constantly throughout our life and it is contextually based on the experience of others. "Young" can mean a time in one's life when they are a child; it can mean a person in their twenties; it can also mean a person in their fifties or sixties depending on who is framing one's age. In my work on identity, I define it as "a relational process through which we understand ourselves/others/groups at any given time in any given place" (Kannen 2013, 179). This is all to say that identity is never a neutral or permanent state of being, but variable and context-dependent. So, what does this mean?

As we discussed in Chapter 1, you might say an identity is something that describes some aspect of who you are—daughter, student, young, or nerdy. Or, you might say something more specific such as woman, queer, Jewish, middle-class, or disabled. In looking at these possibilities, it is important to recognize that all of these categories are being used in relation to other people. We identify ourselves by pointing to some element of who we are that we recognize in relation to someone or something else. While it is true that these identities are constructed, that does not mean that they do not have real and tangible consequences. Identities are central to our sense of self and the meaning that we afford to our bodies, and can (but do not always) provide us with a sense of belonging to communities and the people in our lives. For example, I have used the acronym **2SLGBTQIA+** and the identity **queer**. These terms of identity are in need of definition because they can be so fluid in their meaning. For example, 2SLGBTQIA+ includes, but is not limited to, Two-Spirit, lesbian, gay, bisexual, transgender, queer, intersex, agender, asexual, androgynous, genderfluid, and questioning people. Queer is an umbrella term that I, and many others, use to be as open-ended and inclusive as possible. Queerness is an umbrella term that is both an orientation and a community for those on the 2SLGBTQIA+ spectrum. In Nana's body story, for example, she identified herself as queer.

Identities are also a site of privilege and oppression. The way that we can understand the concept of "normal" shapes our relationship to our bodies and our understandings of ourselves, as well as our relationship to others and their bodies in terms of how we value and treat them. The bodies and identities that are seen to be normal have social privilege. This means that those who are deemed "normal" in society are afforded social advantages, while Others are not. We can see this in many facets of life: how women continually earn less in relation to men; how racialized Black men are more often shot by police than any other people; how employers may see disabled employees as a "problem"—something difficult, something different, something that will cost them more to employ. For those bodies that are unmarked—meaning that they are simply considered to be "normal"—they are often viewed outside of categories of identity: "When a body is emptied of its gender or race, this is a mark of how its position is the privileged norm. Its power emanates from its ability to be seen as just normal, to be without corporeality. Its own gender or race remains invisible; a non-issue" (Puwar 2004, 57). So, what is normal? A "normal body" conforms to a standard expectation; we can only understand normal in relation to the abnormal, the undesirable, the awe-some, and the odd.

Erving Goffman, an influential sociologist, theorized many different elements of our encounters with other people and the potential consequences of these encounters. In his book *Stigma: Notes on the Management of Spoiled Identity* (1963), Goffman argues that bodies are inseparable from the meanings and readings that are put upon them by other people. He claims that "[s]ociety establishes the means of categorizing persons and the complement of attributes felt to be ordinary and natural for members of each of these categories. Social settings establish the categories of persons likely to be encountered there" (2). He makes it clear that these encounters change how we consider ourselves or a stigmatized Other. Goffman says that **stigma** can "be used to refer to an attribute that is deeply discrediting, but it should be seen that a language of relationships, not attributes, is really needed. An attribute that stigmatizes one type of possessor can confirm the usualness of another, and therefore is neither creditable nor discreditable as a thing in itself" (1963, 3). Reminder: a "stigmatized Other," in this instance, is spelled with a capital "O." This is to mark how Other people are those who experience some form of social stigma. Goffman conveys that the Other's appearance enables us to classify those bodies in relation to ourselves in terms of how they "don't fit" with the space that we share and place them as inferior in relation to our own (presumably normal) body. To further this point, Goffman (1963) forcefully claims that "[b]y definition, of course, we believe the person with a stigma is not quite human" (5). When we consider what sorts of people have stigmas, then, we can think of all of those who are positioned outside of "normal" in any given time or place. Throughout history and continuing to today, this list would variously include: women and non-binary folk, racialized people, Indigenous people, disabled people, queer people, working-class people, non-English speakers, the elderly, and so on.

For our purposes here, let's think about what happens when identities intersect, because it is fundamental to remember that they are always intersecting. In Nana's body story, for example, she recognizes her privilege and labels it immediately: "I guess I should start by socially locating myself. I am a white, settler, queer, cis[gender] lady who is a mental health therapist." The identities that Nana is describing are intersecting in the ways that she describes, but her identities also exceed these descriptions because, as with all of us, there are other identities at play as well—her baldness, her age, her clothing, her language, and so on. This makes it clear, then, that these realities are not just true of those with a stigma or who experience oppression; even those categorized as "normal" have intersecting identities. The normality tends to make privileged identities invisible, but it certainly does not mean they are not there.

Stares often occur when identities intersect and appear in ways that confuse a normal expectation of which bodies belong in a certain space and which bodies' very presence alters the expectations of that space. When interactions happen that begin from a stare from one person to another, the situation unfolds in a number of ways. In 1963, Goffman stated, "When normal and stigmatized do in fact enter one another's immediate presence, especially when they there attempt to sustain a joint conversational encounter, there occurs one of the primal scenes of sociology; for, in many cases, these moments will be the ones when the causes and effects of stigma must be directly confronted by both sides" (13). As true today as it was in 1963, confronting the stigma, the Otherness, is what a stare does. Thinking through the reality of staring is where we turn next.

STARING

As we know, stares happen. We stare at things that intrigue, confuse, and alarm us. The people who experience the stare—the staree—however, may have various interpretations about the intent behind it. I know why people stare at my body—it is odd, but what is the underlying aim of the stare? Have they never seen a woman that looks like me before? Are they attracted to me? Are they questioning how I became this way? Are they going to ask me something? For those of us with stareable bodies, we tend to be ready for these encounters because they happen so often. Having said that, as a white woman in Canada, I experience staring through that lens. The staring I receive is not race-based, but due to my unusual height. I have never been asked questions about my race or where I am from. My Canadianness is assumed because my whiteness is a social privilege.

I think that Garland-Thomson (2009) says it best when she notes that "[s]tares are urgent efforts to make the unknown known, to render legible something that seems at first glance incomprehensible. In this way, staring becomes a starer's quest to know and a staree's opportunity to be known" (15). To reiterate, as the concept of "race" is a social construction, it "is best understood in terms of social and political processes of racialization, or race-making" (Baum 2006, 10). In other words, **racialization** is the process that causes relationships, social practices, or groups to have racial meanings in society. The limits of language, Satzewich and Liodakis (2013) point out, means that we use the term "race" to mean a wide variety of things, and "despite the analytical problems with the concept of 'race,' Canadian society still tries to measure and quantify 'race' and 'racial diversity'" (20). Bianca Gonzalez-Sobrino and Devon R. Goss (2019) elaborate on the concept of racialization by stating:

> Theories of race and racism seek to understand how race operates in … society and how racial inequality is created and maintained. "Racialization" as a concept has been used as a part of critical race theory to understand the process through which racial meaning is attached to something that is to perceived to be "unracial" or devoid of racial meaning. (505)

The connection between staring and racialized bodies is fundamentally connected to how certain bodies are not seen to fit within the spaces they occupy. Spaces, for example, have no inherent race to them; we create racial meanings in certain spaces based on cultural expectations of what sorts of people we expect to find there.

In Desmond Cole's *The Skin We're In*, Cole articulates how Canada has a racism problem, specifically in terms of state violence toward and over-incarceration of Black and Indigenous people of colour (BIPOC). Cole (2020) says that "[w]hite supremacy, which informs and fuels anti-Black racism, is an insatiable force. White supremacy is never personal, never individual, never isolated. … We are talking about a system of power that seeks to benefit white people above all others" (8). As a Black woman who lives and works in a predominantly white city, Rae tells the story of an experience walking up a staircase surrounded by glass walls in her former workplace. The transparency of the staircase meant that people could watch her walk up and down the stairs from a boardroom. When she described these experiences to her white colleagues and friends, they often dismissed her.

Rae: I know when I am being stared at and yet everyone would say to me, "Oh, but how are you sure that they are staring? Maybe you just looked and they looked back." And I'm like, "No, you can tell because when you look and you catch eyes with someone that you don't want to catch eyes with, then you look away. And then when I glance back, they're still looking." They are literally tracking me walking up the staircase. And, in my mind, I'm wondering, "Why are you staring at me? Like, do you stare at every single person that walks up the staircase?" I don't know, because I'm not just another person walking up the staircase. I'm a Black woman walking up. It's just so uncomfortable. It's just like, you know, going on with the business of my day, and it's just like, it feels like they are staring to ask: "Why are you here?" Right there. That's it. I'm thinking that they are thinking, "You don't belong."

In our conversation, Rae describes how people often stare at her and how it makes her feel excluded from even the possibility of belonging. Nirmal Puwar (2004) argues that when certain bodies enter into spaces where they are seen as not belonging, they are "space invaders." She claims that there is a dissonance or disconnect caused "by the arrival of women and racialized minorities in privileged occupational spaces," and it "unleashes shock and surprise. Their entry causes disorientation and terror. The threat they are seen to pose amplifies their presence. As 'space invaders' they represent a potential organizational terror. They are thus highly visible bodies that by their mere presence invite suspicion and surveillance" (Puwar 2004, 54). The stares that Rae has received in predominantly white workplaces are not isolated. They happen over and over again.

Rae's experience also speaks to the ways that racialization functions to place her as Other in relation to the seemingly white homogeneity of her city and broader Canadian society. As Emma Dabiri (2019) says, "[a]s an isolated 'mixed-race' or black individual in a predominantly white environment, you become a cipher, a representation of coming anarchy. The barbarians have breached the gates and you are the manifestations of all the fantasies, fears and desires that have been absorbed by a population fed a steady diet of racist discourse" (9). In speaking of her encounters with racist stares toward her body, Rae says, "I'm tired.

I'll be walking home and first comes the stare and then there's an interaction that happens. I actually don't want to be followed home or pursue it further. So, sometimes I don't respond to a racist question. I don't want to have to always say something or do something back." Rae and Dabiri are expressing that their positioning as Black women represents something far beyond darker skin tone. Blackness is equated with a history of difference, fear, and a systemic belief in **white supremacy**. "The white body is not subject to the same regulatory procedures as the body racialized as black" (Dabiri 2019, 26). For example, a dishevelled white person may read as chic or bohemian, but a "shabby" Black person could be read as wild and threatening. "With such perception comes the use of regulatory power against the black body, perhaps resulting in arrest, or even death" (Dabiri 2019, 26). These expectations have become all too commonplace as racial profiling proliferates in North America, by individuals and institutions.

Rae recalls a racist experience that she had as a child when she was living in a predominantly white area of the United Kingdom.

Rae: I remember I'd be riding my bike around the subdivisions or whatever and they would say something like, "Go back where you came from, *Paki*," and I remember telling my mom and she explained that to them everybody who looks different becomes lumped into one group of people. And we had another incident where there was some holiday where everybody does fireworks. We were walking back from a friend's house—my mother and my sister and me—and these kids in the neighborhood set some fireworks off right next to us and ran away. We had sparks on us. My mom called the police and they said that they didn't think we needed to be afraid. We were afraid. I haven't had anything like that here, but there have been many everyday life instances of racism because it is embedded here too.

In her final comment, Rae is referring to how Canada is built upon a colonial narrative—one that continues to be written. This land was violently stolen from Indigenous peoples, and the slavery of Black people is a historical reality that many of us are not taught in school, but the effects of this racism underlie contemporary relations in Canada. As

Cole (2020) says, "the struggle for Black life in modern-day Canada is a living struggle, as urgent today as it has ever been" (17). Further, there is a Canadian belief of being well-meaning that pervades our nationalist narratives, but this peace and goodwill—even when individuals and institutions claim to "mean well" in their relations with bodies that are "unexpected"—does not excuse the damage or, in many instances, the violence that this "goodwill" can cause.

THE WELL-MEANING STRANGER

We have all experienced them. The stranger who comes up to you to say … something. Every person that I interviewed for this book has been approached by someone—with good intentions or not—to comment on their body.

> **Nana:** So, some of the interactions that I've had, and there have been many with people in the category … I guess we could call it "the well-meaning stranger." Sometimes, I would almost want people to look at me and actually ask me, like, just ask me whatever it is because I know you're uncomfortable. The stare is worse.

Nana names these people "the well-meaning stranger" because she believes that the comments she receives are essentially coming from a place of sympathy or empathy. As a reminder, Nana chooses to shave her head because of her hair-pulling and skin-picking. She has had people approach her to tell her that they have sympathy for her because she must be going through cancer treatment, struggling with alopecia (a condition that causes hair loss), or that she seems to be having a "Britney moment." In case you are not familiar, Britney Spears famously grabbed a razor and shaved off all of her hair in view of the paparazzi in 2007 because she was said to have had a mental and emotional "collapse."

The gaze of the stranger is clearly tied to the discussion of staring that we have had, but thinking about the stranger in particular adds a new element. Staring, while impactful, happens at a distance. We can feel the stare, but it can be privately acknowledged and experienced without further interaction. You can think to yourself: "Oh, that person is staring at me." The well-meaning stranger, on the other hand, is someone who moves past the stare and starts a conversation about why they are staring at you. Nana expresses this experience in describing how she was approached by a stranger shortly after she decided to no longer wear a wig to cover her shaved head.

Nana: I was walking my dog and just like letting my bald head just be in the air. I was practising some exposure to not wearing a hat out in public and letting my bald spots be out to see that the world doesn't end. And that I can live and survive that. So, I challenged myself to walk around the block with my dog with my hat off. And on this day where I was challenging myself, a woman, with her partner and their kids were in the car, had the power to pull the car off to the side of the road where I was walking. She rolled down her window, and she was like, "Hey," and I thought she needed directions or something. So, I walked over to the car. And she says, "I have alopecia too." And I froze and didn't speak. And she went on, "I'm sorry for you, but I want to let you know that I also have alopecia. And by the way, it's so brave that you're just showing the world that you have it. But if you wanted to know the names of some great naturopaths in town, I've had a lot of success with my hair loss through like naturopathic remedies," and I had to stop her. And I was like, "Number one, this is really uncomfortable for me. Thank you for your well-meaning intentions, but this is really uncomfortable for me." And her kids were in the back, staring at me, and then I said, "I actually don't have alopecia. I have hair loss for a different reason." And then she didn't know what to do. Right? She just sort of stared at me and was like, "Oh, I'm sorry." And then she said, "But you know what? You should really look into those naturopaths anyway. Because they might help with whatever you have."

I think that this is a very good example of where interactions in public—regardless of how well-meaning a person is—demonstrate that what we say and do have consequences. As Nana and I continued talking about this experience, she articulated the way this momentary interaction made her feel and how those feelings remained.

Nana: It was like so weird and I felt so jarred by that and then really shaky and I felt really surveilled. Then, right away, I started thinking about who else is looking at me and watching me and thinking that I need some sort of intervention, right? Because most people would not pull over their car to offer me vitamins or whatever. And then, it was this weird moment where I didn't feel like my body was all mine. All of a sudden, my body wasn't just private. For me. It was public for others. And yeah, because most of the time, like eighty per cent of the time, I go about my day, totally not remembering that I have bald spots on my head. And then it might be the stare or comment from a stranger or a child pointing that reminds me of my difference.

When Nana says "I didn't feel like my body was all mine," she is pointing to a larger question of who is allowed to keep their body private. Why are some bodies positioned as available to the public, while others have a right to privacy and security? People who look unusual become accustomed to these unwanted interactions and are forced to develop strategies in order to make the situations liveable. This reality is one that we will continually return to throughout the book as there is no right way to handle these moments. Nana was very honest in saying that she felt uncomfortable, but that's not an easy thing to do. We are actually rarely honest when we are made uncomfortable. We live in a society where, when people ask how we are, the expected answer is "Good. How are you?" followed by another "Good." The multiple "goods" are often not true representations of how we feel, but we are taught not to share our truth with other people so as to not burden them. In the moment where Nana said she was uncomfortable, she took charge of the situation: "Rather than passively wilting under intrusive and discomforting stares, a staree can take charge of a staring situation, using charm, friendliness, humor, formidability, or perspicacity to reduce interpersonal tension and enact a positive self-representation" (Garland-Thomson 2009, 84). Although Nana did not bare her truth, as it were, she did make it clear that she was struggling with the intentions of the stranger and, as a staree, took charge of the situation.

It is important to emphasize here that a question from a stranger is not inherently unacceptable, but for the folks in this book, it is also not an isolated experience. A well-intentioned question exists amongst hundreds—if not thousands—of interactions that stareable, stigmatized bodies encounter. Over the course of one's life, it can become—as Rae said—tiring. Goffman (1963) claims that when a stranger approaches us, we develop displeasure because our Otherness becomes the obvious reason for the interaction; we then feel exposed, isolated, and realize that "normal" people either feel bad for us or feel curious about how and why we exist at all.

Nana articulated the metaphorical choices of a stareable person when the well-meaning stranger approaches her. She pictures it as four doors.

> Door number one: Graciously accept whatever just happened and move on with your day.

> Door number two: This is an educational door. If you walk through it, you teach the stranger what your truth is in whatever way that you feel comfortable.

> Door number three: Be a bit grumpy or even shocked. Give more details about your body than seems socially acceptable and, by doing so, hopefully dissuade them from coming up to other people.

> Door number four: Acknowledge that this is uncomfortable and say something like "Please, in the future, I would ask you to not comment on a stranger's appearance if they don't give you permission" and then leave.

As a therapist and an extremely empathetic person, it is clear that Nana has thought through her engagements with strangers on many levels, but even she acknowledges the complexity of the door you choose.

Nana: I always want to leave a little bit of a legacy in that person so that they won't do that to the next person they see with a visible difference, but I am the first to acknowledge that I haven't necessarily built up my warrior armor quite yet. I am certainly not a consistent and constant educator, but I am working on it.

No one should be expected to have a perfect reaction to a stranger. Before we move on, consider the four above options and ask yourself: How might you respond if a stranger was staring at you and then approached you to ask, for example, "Can I touch your hair?"

HAIR

Our hair is serious. "It's our glory, our nemesis, our history, our sexuality, our religion, our vanity, our joy, and our mortality. It's true that there are many things in life that matter more than hair, but few that matter in quite these complicated, energizing, and interconnected ways" (Benedict 2015, xvii). Our hair is political. For example, while an absence of hair for women can be a signal of supposed illness (as in Nana's experience), intentional baldness can also be a sign of fierce resistance to feminine norms.

As a reminder, gender refers to the socially constructed roles, behaviours, activities, and attributes that relate to understandings of masculinities and femininities in every society. Hair is extremely gendered. The politics of hair go well beyond whether one has hair or not. The kinds of hair we have—how it looks, how it feels, its thickness or thinness, where it is, where it isn't, its colour(s), and style—these are all embedded within gendered *and* racialized assumptions of hair goodness and desirability. "And there are the other questions that hair leads to as well, about femininity, questions that haunt women of all shades, hues, and races. Why do we have to live under the tyranny of a global doctrine that posits femininity in the length and straightness of a woman's hair?" (Golden 2015, 30). Marita Golden (2015) argues that Black women—like all women—"live imprisoned by a cultural belief system about beauty and hair whose time should have passed" (31). Here, she is referring to how systemic privileging of white femininity—pale skin, European features, straight-long hair—has been and is still upheld as the global ideal of beauty. She goes on to say: "Like everything else about Black folk, Black people's—and especially Black women's—hair is knotted and gnarled by issues of race, politics, history, and pride" (Golden 2015, 19).

In speaking about her hair, Rae expressed that other people's interest in her hair—because she is a Black woman—is a daily occurrence.

Rae: Just today, I had someone ask to touch my hair. I let her—I don't know why. I guess because she was younger? She said she loved my hair. So that was nice! On the flip side, I've let someone touch my hair and they're like, "Oh, it's so soft. I didn't think it'd be soft" and like, it's hair. What do you think it was gonna feel like? I'm laughing while talking to you about it, but ugh … I can't stand that. Or just even the questions about how I do my hair. Or, "How does it feel?" … regardless of if I wear my hair out or if I have it wrapped, there are days where I wake up and I don't want to have to have a conversation about my hair, my head wrap or whatever. And I try to figure out what I can do that's gonna attract the least amount of attention today. And, it never works. It's big and curly, but like *more*. It's not quite like an afro. I have rather coily hair, but the coils are like really tight—they call it 4A hair.

Both Rae and Nana have complex relationships to their hair. Rae's relationship can be explored through gender and race, while Nana's relationship through gender and a disability lens. By disability lens, I refer to the ways that Nana's shaved head is symbolic of her experience with the medicalization of her hair-pulling. In considering disability, we need to understand that "[d]isability activists fiercely declare that it's not our bodies that need curing. Rather, it is ableism—disability oppression, as reflected in high unemployment rates, lack of access, gawking, substandard education, being forced to live in nursing homes and back rooms, being seen as childlike and asexual—that needs changing" (Clare 2001, 360). This perspective recognizes that many people—Nana included—do not identify as having a disability because of the common ways that disability labels position people as *less than* or suffering, which are stereotypes Nana resists. Garland-Thomson (1997) helps define disability by claiming that "disability is a representation, a cultural interpretation of physical transformation or configuration, and a comparison of bodies that structures social relations and institutions. Disability, then, is the attribution of corporeal deviance—not so much a property of bodies as a product of cultural rules about what bodies should be or do" (6). Later, she extends this idea to explain why a disability identity is so challenging for some people to take on: "The refusal to claim disability identity is in part due to a lack of ways to understand or talk about disability that are not oppressive" (Garland-Thomson 2011, 35). It is important to recognize the uniqueness of this relationship to an identity—choosing to disidentify is a choice and one that many people may not understand, but this also reminds us of the social nature of identities. They are parts of ourselves that seem so natural, but are crafted and created out of various understandings, and our relationship to those understandings can change and take different shapes as we move through life.

As Nana states, "I'm not distressed by my hair-pulling, and I don't believe that I experience any impairments, so in that way I decided that I actually don't have trichotillomania even though I compulsively pull my hair out." So, I am framing the discussion of Nana and her hair-pulling within the context of a disability conversation because the theories and ideas that help to understand her compulsion are best expressed through a disability studies lens. Having said that, the way that Nana identifies is not within the language of disability. Her relationship to hair is unique—in her words, isolating—because of the way that she frames her hair-pulling. For example, Nana describes why she began shaving her head as an act of self-care.

Nana: I will just name my experience relating to a visibility piece. So, folks who compulsively pull out their hair most often opt to invisibilize that reality. In an act of self-protection, most opt to cover up their balding areas, through maybe a certain hairstyle or headscarves or hats or wigs. I think it was about five years ago, I decided to shave my head because the amount of hair that I was pulling out was taking up a ton of real estate on my head. The repetitiveness of the behavior was causing me a lot of pain in my hands and fingers and my scalp. And five years ago or so, I was also grappling with a ton of shame. So, I could not cover up the balding area anymore. If you think about the size of a yarmulke, like, that's sitting on someone's head? That was about how much hair was gone. So, from literally like the tops of my ears in a semicircle around my crown of my head, that hair was all gone.

And the rest of my hair was longer than my shoulders. So, the baldness appeared very starkly. I reached a breaking point and I shaved my head to gain a sense of relief over this behavior. And I immediately bought a wig because at the time it was my belief that nobody can see this about me. No one can know that I've shaved my head because of this. So, I bought a wig. And so I wore that wig for two years.

For quite some time, Nana chose to cover her hair-pulling by wearing hats or a wig. The covering, of course, did not change her reality; rather, it simply attempted to hide from the public what she was doing with her body in private. While covering can be an escape from stares, the issue with covering is that it forfeits Nana's ability to be recognized for who she is and how she resists the norm.

Nana: I get it. There is supposed to be hair there; why isn't there hair there? And the bald patches being, you know, irregular for a time, not as much now but for a long period of time, I was struggling a lot with skin-picking on my scalp. So, if there was like a bump or an ingrown hair, you know, you get like little pimples or whatever on your scalp. I would just pick the shit out of it and then get these big scabs, big sores. I feel like that was likely very hard for people to see. Questioning whether I was ill or diseased. A full head of hair is often socially and even medically associated with good health. And like, I don't know if you've heard people say like, "I was so crazy. I was so nervous … I was pulling my hair out." There is a belief that women, but only women, if they have no hair they must not be well. Mentally or otherwise.

As described previously, on Nana's first day walking around without a head covering, she had an interaction that has stayed with her. This is not uncommon. Remember Rae's story about being stared at in her former workplace? It is in these ways that these encounters linger—the comments made, the decisions on how to respond, what was said and what could have been said, which all fuel how we experience the next inevitable interaction.

Rae and Nana—as all women—experience hair in complicated ways. How they feel about their hair changes regularly, but these feelings are also driven by their interactions about hair with others. As we move forward, Rae and Nana's experiences help to enable a deeper understanding of the stories that follow. In the next stories, you will meet Kali and Alice, whose stories help frame how bodies are both private and public (sexualized) spaces.

KEY WORDS

Queer; Racialization; Stigma; White supremacy; 2SLGBTQIA+

QUESTIONS FOR REFLECTION AND DISCUSSION

1. What is the role of our bodily privacy when our bodies are in public? What kinds of protections do you expect and want for your body? How are limits defined?
2. What do you see as most significant about the way that Nana and Rae were visually interpreted by Damian? How did you imagine them based on their stories?
3. Some concepts, like "queer," have been reclaimed and transformed over time. This has caused some people to feel conflicted about their use. Are there any words or concepts that have meanings that are challenging for you to engage with? Why?

CHAPTER 3

Our Bodies as Private and Public (Sexualized) Spaces

Body Story: Kali

I think people think I am a lot less independent or self-sufficient than I actually am. I am brave as fuck. I'm actually always brave and that gets complicated.

—Kali

My interview with Kali felt dream-like. It's difficult to describe her; she is someone who exceeds simplistic characterizations. Kali, describing herself, says: "I'm a tiny, feminine, brown woman. I live in Southern Ontario and work for the federal government now, but I also worked as a stripper for almost four years. I still identify as a sex worker, actually. And I have a master's degree in social work with a specialization in social policy administration. I did an undergraduate degree in international development, specializing in gender. I teach pole dancing. I am almost a full-fledged coach. And, in my spare time, I walk dogs." It is an amazing array of information to process.

Kali is intensely committed to everything that she does and, yet, she also has a deep ambivalence toward many of her experiences. When she describes her family, this ambivalence is tangible.

Kali: My public bravery in the face of racism and fear is so complicated because I was raised in a very unstable family situation to begin with. I was hyper-sheltered because my mom is from a very strict South Asian culture where women don't walk down the street by themselves and you always have a man when you are navigating public spaces as a woman. So, I'm a very independent person. I've always fought for that. And I've always fought to not be afraid. Fuck the patriarchy and all that stuff. I love nighttime and I love exploring and I am such an adventurer, and I was like, "No, this fear my parents have instilled in me isn't real." And then I go outside and I get punched in the face by a racist. And I get followed home. Somebody even threw something at me once. I am now always braced in public. But I have also believed that for my whole life, I've been told a lie based on fear. I firmly believed that I didn't need to be afraid. But now I see that in some ways my parents were not wrong. They didn't overdo it. Because, I wonder if my mom experienced this as well. And she just never had a healthy way to cope with it or process it. Still, I'm like—fuck the patriarchy, and a nighttime explorer—but I hear their voices of warning for my sexualized, brown body.

The desire to resist the influence of your family on your sense of self and the world, while simultaneously recognizing that there is truth to their words, embodies a powerful, in-between space that Kali occupies. As a 27-year-old bisexual mixed race woman—her mother Sri Lankan, her father Irish—Kali lives in the in-between: she is a sex worker, a government employee, a body modifier, *and* recognizes the pressures on women's bodies to modify. She embraces this fluidity and says, "What does the world expect? Do you expect me to just sit here and be miserable or secure and, like, not engage beyond those expectations whatsoever? I refuse."

Kali describes herself in ways that are consistently political, but she has an air of sassiness to her as well. In describing some of the body modification she has done—particularly in terms of using fillers on her face—she says:

Kali: So I'm very open about it. I think it's important to admit different things. I always tell people and kind of be light-hearted about it, like, "Yeah, I got my lips done." My lips were always very full. I love that bottom lip, but I didn't love my skinny little top lip and so I wanted to just bump it up so I could, you know, have a companion for the other one. I always tell them, I got one fake lip and one real one. [*laughs*]

In our conversation, Kali told me that she is so open because she wants to take some power away from certain body modifiers, like hair dye and skin treatments, and to try to normalize the ways that women want to look and how they can make these decisions for themselves.

Kali: People, generally, are quite positive about it, but also because I've done my face in a way that is generally considered socially acceptable because I don't look quote–unquote "too plastic." Right? Although, it shouldn't matter. Like if I want to look like Barbie, it shouldn't matter. Because it's about me, right? ... Even my dad, he's taken me to these appointments before and been like, "This is fine, but if you go any further than this, you're gonna look like a duck and I just don't want you looking like a duck." And I'm like, and I actually said this to him: "What if I wanted to fucking look like a duck? This isn't for you."

Kali
Damian Mellin, 2020

Within this illustration, my goal was to show the depth of time. From the past, which is in the background, including images of stripper clubs to queer clubs to Kali being in the forefront as someone who is in a powerful position. Kali's story just seems so powerful and also dangerous, so I wanted to ensure that her illustration has an over-the-top edgy vibe.—Damian Mellin

Body Story: Alice

It's interesting in the way that people will think that existing in public automatically involves some kind of invitation for comment.
　　—Alice

Alice is eloquent and guarded. In our conversation, her voice often remained quiet, but the strength of her words is what resonated with me most.

Alice: So, I've definitely had people kind of come into my space and ask intrusive things. I think the one I get the most questions on are about my tattoos and the flock of ravens falling up or flying up my bicep. People seem to really focus in on these. Not sure why, but then a lot of people ask me about the fleur-de-lis on my breast. So those are kind of the two big ones that seem to attract the most attention.

Alice describes her experience of privilege in many ways—enrolled in a graduate program at the University of British Columbia, being tall, white, passing as cisgender—but her experiences in public are often fraught with complexity. "I'm very lucky, generally speaking, because people just look at me and assume that I am a woman, they don't necessarily assume that I'm trans. I think a lot of the time I am assumed to be a cis woman, which is lucky in regards to my safety, but it is a double erasure of my gender and queerness … yet it is a point of privilege." She identifies as moving between androgyny and femininity, but uses "she" as her preferred pronoun. At 22, Alice is the youngest person that I interviewed, but she is so connected to her body and how she experiences her body that it felt like I was talking to a scholar well beyond her years.

Similar to Rae, Alice's hair is also a point of interaction with the public. "To be honest, I have had a lot of people just kind of constantly touching my hair. I think it is because it is soft and it is an unusual colour because of the red gingerness of it. So, people seem fascinated with it and will consciously comment or touch it or play with it, which—if they are my friends, I don't mind. With strangers? It's a little, well, strange." Her use of the word "strange" here is putting it mildly. She describes very invasive questions about her body, which border on violent (these are discussed in more depth later in this chapter). For Alice, her reflections on her gendered encounters speak to the expectations that others have of bodies and their attempt to place them: "I think one of the most interesting shifts for me since I transitioned has been that I always received the: "Oh, you're so tall, you should play basketball!" But, now, it is, "Oh, you're so tall, you should model!" There's a very interesting kind of dichotomy there as to what people expect from bodies depending on how they're gendered." Alice spoke of these gendered dynamics through digital spaces (in which she is active), fashion, exoticization, and fetishization.

As our conversation went on, it became clearer that Alice's relationship to her body is still in a process of transition. She says: "At times, the sheer act of being visible in public makes me panic. I have moments where I've actually had to leave work because I've had panic attacks just because of being physically present. And that's mostly because I have body dysmorphi[c] disorder, which means that I have a tendency to hyperfixate on elements of my physical appearance that either aren't there or are drastically exaggerated in my head." She describes this dysphoria as having been "pretty potent for a year or so," and explains that it has escalated now that there is more conversation about her body with others and constant reminders of her physical presence.

Alice is articulate in discussing the ways that her body is read. In a moment where we were discussing how we both met our partners on Twitter, I decided to ask: "When you're out with your partner in Vancouver, does the interaction with strangers change at all?" Her answer squarely tackles some of why she is so attuned to discussing identity.

Alice: It becomes interesting because not only is my partner also trans, but she's a butch lesbian. So, we end up in a lot of situations of people kind of—or at least, I noticed a lot of people kind of looking at us, and I can tell they're trying to figure out, you know, if we're a gay couple or lesbian couple or a straight couple, whatever we are, and it's interesting. We are intriguing to them because I think that they have that need to classify us. Or at least they want to classify our presentation. I think we actually defy whatever notions they may have. Yeah, I think that's definitely been an interesting kind of point of interest and discovery. It has been, navigating that.

Alice
Damian Mellin, 2020

For this piece, I wanted to reclaim famous B movies that had an emphasis on power-
ful, strong women. Movies such as Attack of the 50 Foot Woman *were etched in*
my mind when Alice talked about being the very tall woman in a very small town.
—Damian Mellin

Body Theories: Responding to Kali and Alice

SEXUALIZED SPACES

Sexualization, fetishization of the exotic, and a fierce sense of embodiment are what bind Kali and Alice's body stories together. They both describe the deeply gendered and sexualized ways that their bodies are read in public (as well as racialized in Kali's experience) and how these readings contribute to their understandings of themselves. Before introducing a discussion of our sexualized bodies as public and private spaces, this chapter will engage with key ideas of sexuality—namely, practical and theoretical understandings, as well as fetishization and exoticism. Lastly, we will explore how these ideas connect to what it means to be sex critical.

The role of space—the private and the public—is deeply connected to bodies. Particularly in the world of COVID-19, we talk of physical distance, social distance, and personal space more than any other time that has come before. These, however, are not new concepts. In Robert Sommer's (2007) seminal text *Personal Space: The Behavioral Basis of Design*, he describes the role of personal and private space in ways that are key to our understandings. He states, "Personal space refers to an area with invisible boundaries surrounding a person's body into which intruders may not come" (41). Sommer goes on to say that "[p]ersonal space is not necessarily spherical in shape, nor does it extend equally in all directions. (People are able to tolerate closer presence of a stranger at their sides than directly in front)" (41). Our personal space "has been likened to a snail shell, a soap bubble, an aura, and 'breathing room'" (41). While we are inherently social creatures, we still seek privacy in our lives—in our homes, at work, in public places, in our bodies. Generally, we do not want this privacy invaded. Navigating these invasions, particularly when they relate to gender and sexuality, is something many people experience every day.

What is "the public"? Michael Warner (2002) debates this question at length in his work. Warner states:

> [T]he public is a kind of social totality. … It might be the people organized as the nation, the commonwealth, the city, the state, or some other community. It might be very general, as in Christendom or humanity. But in each case the public, as a people, is thought to include everyone within the field in question. … A public can also be a second thing: a concrete audience, a crowd witnessing itself in visible space, as with a theatrical public. Such a public also has a sense of totality, bounded by the event or by the shared physical space. A performer on stage knows where her public is, how big it is, where its boundaries are, and what the time of its common existence is. A crowd at a sports event, a concert, or a riot might be a bit blurrier around the edges, but still knows itself by knowing where and when it is assembled in common visibility and common action. (49–50)

When we refer to the public, we can mean all of those people outside of our circle, outside of what we consider private, outside of where our safe boundaries lie. It is both conceptual and real to us. This framing is important to understand the role of our bodies as both private and public *things* and *experiences*.

SEX, GENDER, AND SEXUALITY

Before we dive into a discussion of bodies as sexualized spaces and places, it seems necessary to explore the role of sexuality within Western culture. When we consider the ways that gender and race are constructed, we can extend this discussion to sexuality as well. Feona Attwood defines **sexuality** as referring to "all erotically significant aspects of social life and social being—desires, practices, relationships and identities, as well as sexual interests, acts, expressions and/or experiences" (2018, 6). Sexuality intersects with race and gender in inextricable ways. Margo DeMello says, "everything related to sex—and by that, we refer to your biological **sex**, the sexual relations that you may have, and your sexual identity and orientation—is shaped by, and understood through, the lens of culture" (2014, 137). Our everyday socialization involves exposure to social definitions that distinguish the sexual from the non-sexual, label some forms of sexuality as acceptable and others abhorrent, and construct sexual scripts for masculinities and femininities. These "rules" are usually conveyed through our language, but they are also conveyed through social behaviours, such as staring.

Sexuality is an often misunderstood—or variously understood— term. The role of sexuality in our life reflects one of the major axes through which we understand ourselves and others. Sexuality, as a core identity for each of us, is a social power dynamic where people can be oppressed, liberated, or exist somewhere in between. Historically, feminists have been concerned with sexuality because women's sexuality has been under the social and cultural control of those in power, namely patriarchal rule. Areas of concern for feminists in terms of sexuality remain largely in terms of women's sexual objectification and sexual exploitation in the media and society (see Agustín 2007; Egan 2013), control of reproduction (Solinger 2019; Ross 2017), sex work (Albury 2017; Chateauvert 2013), sex education (Allen 2005; Allen and Rasmussen 2017), sexual representation and diversity online (Nixon and Düsterköft 2018), and the ways in which the wide variety of expressions of female sexuality can be empowering to women when they are freely chosen (Attwood 2018).

Michel Foucault's contributions to the study of institutions and power relations, as well as the body and its relation to power, are what I aim to address here. Foucault encourages the understanding that the "lived body" is both a biological unit and a social actor. Bodies have physiological potential and limitations, yet they can surpass their materiality through their social embodiment; in other words, the social aspects of who we are (or how we appear to one another) foster meanings in ways that mere physiology is incapable of explaining. Foucault (1984) claims that the body, in its presentation, exemplifies how notions of authenticity are constructed and reproduced in an attempt to obscure how it is not possible to achieve the intended expressions. This body, then, is not a cohesive unity, but rather a collection of expressions that can only try to convey a "real" or authentic self. Furthermore, for Foucault, the body is a subject of power; by this I mean that the body is both found within, and is an expression of, discourses and practices of power. As I introduced in Chapter 1, power is—at all times—intermingled with every facet of society. Power "is not something that is acquired, seized, or shared, something that one holds on to or allows to slip away; power is exercised from innumerable points, in the interplay of nonegalitarian and mobile relations" (Foucault 1990, 94). Implying both a hierarchy of social relations and the transitory nature of those relations, Foucault insists that each individual has power; power enables and constrains and, thus, it can be enacted and resisted. While this seems like a positive connotation in relation to our individual power, it must also be acknowledged that this power is never outside of various collective powers, which often subjugate and marginalize those individuals who do not conform to the ideals of the more powerful collective.

Power is theorized by many scholars as a means to explain social inequality, but Foucault's contribution is particularly notable with regard to his concept of bio-power. As a political strategy, bio-power refers to exercising power over Other bodies, as it is an "explosion of numerous and diverse techniques for achieving the subjugation of bodies and the control of populations" (Foucault 1990, 140). This concept helps to explain the ways in which bodies come to be regulated and separated via practices of individualization and normalization; it is not merely that some bodies are normal and some are abnormal; rather it is the very existence of the norm that encourages the disciplining of bodies into a binary of those who are able or unable to conform to that norm (Foucault 2007).

Western politics *and* culture have simultaneously repressed open discussion about women's biology *and* sex. This reality has frequently obscured, misinformed, withheld, and abused information about the place of bio-functional realities and health in women's lives. These smokescreens also allow the binary of male/female to remain firmly in place and unquestioned, when in fact there is not only tremendous gender diversity, there is also genetic variation and biological diversity within bodies. When filling out a document such as a job application or school registration form you are often asked to provide your name, address, phone number, birth date, and sex or gender. But have you ever been asked to provide your sex *and* your gender? As with many people, it may not have occurred to you that sex and gender are not the same.

As noted by Attwood (2018), sex is a wide-ranging term that refers to physical or physiological differences between males and females, including both primary sex characteristics (the reproductive system) and secondary characteristics such as height and muscularity. However, "sex also refers to particular acts—summed up in the idea that we can 'have sex.' A broader range of things are seen as 'sexy': a particular quality or look, the ability to excite desire and stimulate attraction" (7). The distinction between sex and gender is key to being able to examine gender and sexuality as social identities rather than biological variables. Anne Fausto-Sterling (2000) underscores how gender and sex must be understood as separate and the constructed nature of that difference:

> Labeling someone a man or a woman is a social decision. We may use scientific knowledge to help us make the decision, but only our beliefs about gender—not science—can define our sex. Furthermore, our beliefs about gender affect what kinds of knowledge scientists produce about sex in the first place. (3)

Attwood (2018) characterizes gender orientations as follows:

Trans: refers to those who move away from the gender they were assigned at birth.

Cisgender: refers to people who are not trans and who remain in the gender they were assigned at birth.

Androgynous: people whose identities incorporate aspects of gender associated with women and men.

Agender: people whose identities are not based on gender.

Gender fluid: people who move between genders.

Pangender: people who move between multiple genders.

Third gender: people who consider themselves to be of an additional gender. (10)

While this is not a complete list (because there are forms of gender expressions that vary cross-culturally and historically), these definitions provide a sense of the possibilities of gender beyond the limited understanding of man or woman that we are most often presented with. We can see the ways gender is a fundamental guiding principle in our lives from birth. Not only are we gendered consumers, but gender is embedded in our legal codes, social institutions, and our language(s).

Gender is also a fundamental guiding principle of our **heteronormative** society. Ingraham (2017) claims that the dominance of heterosexuality is reflected in how heterosexuality is both an ideology and a social institution that fosters the idea that heterosexuality is both natural and normal. It is also through heteronormative discursive practices that 2SLGBTQIA+ lives are marginalized socially and politically and, as a result, are often invisible within social spaces such as schools. Heteronormative values are not inherent or natural, despite the belief that they are. However, it is actually **homonormativity**, which is perhaps less talked about but more embedded in bodily practices that encourages 2SLGBTQIA+ people to attempt to mimic heterosexuality and all of its created characteristics and assumptions. For example, a homonormative lens enforces and rewards those 2SLGBTQIA+ people that are able to conform to the idea that there are only two (cis)genders— male and female. In this way, stereotypes of masculine bodies (physically strong, participating in hegemonic masculine activities, etc.) and feminine bodies (taking up little space, feminine appearance, participating in care work, etc.) will be rewarded for their ability to pass as "normal" in heteronormative spaces.

While we have discussed sexuality above, its definition has not yet been offered. Sexuality "may refer to *orientation* or *preference* (the way someone experiences attraction and desire), or to identity (how they define themselves sexually)" (Attwood 2018, 7). Attwood also outlines some common sexual orientations and identities. Here are those that are most commonly in use (2018, 10):

Asexual: describes people who may not experience sexual attraction or arousal, or people who experience these things without feeling the need to act them out sexually or with a partner.

Bisexual: describes people who may be attracted to more than one gender, or for whom gender isn't a factor in who they are attracted to.

BDSM or kink: refers to people who engage in sexual practices that emphasize exchanges of power, restriction of movement, or intense sensations.

Homosexual: refers to people who are attracted to people of the same gender.

Heterosexual: refers to people who are attracted to people who they understand to be of the "opposite" gender (men to women and women to men).

Monosexual: refers to people who are attracted to people of only one gender.

These definitions help to make clear what elements of sexuality exist and can also always be challenged, added to, and elaborated in order to challenge heteronormative discussions. Ingraham (2017) refers to key feminist theorists, such as Adrienne Rich, who have argued that heterosexuality is made to seem compulsory, even though it is "contrived, constructed and a taken-for-granted institution which serves the interests of male dominance" (75). In the following section, we explore the role of our bodies as sexualized spaces and places.

OUR BODIES AS SEXUALIZED SPACES AND PLACES

Many of the examples in this book reflect an invasion of personal space. As Sommer (2007) notes, "[d]espite increased awareness, most people still accept invaded space as a consequence of urban life. They don't like the intrusion, but resist provoking an uncertain response from someone who has already displayed bad manners" (57). I would characterize Kali and Alice as both being **sex positive** as they are open-minded and promote healthy dialogue about the diversity and plurality of sex and sexuality. While they are incredibly self-reflective on their experiences of sexuality, this does not negate the invasions that they have experienced—physically and verbally. It is also key to note that just because they are able to expertly assess and reflect upon the sexualized experiences they have had does not mean the effects of these encounters are not ongoing and potentially debilitating.

As a reminder, intersectionality refers to the ways that our identities are never disconnected from each other. Intersectional analyses suggest that biological, social, and cultural categories such as gender, race, sexuality, and other axes of identity interact and intersect on multiple and often simultaneous levels. While Kimberlé Crenshaw's (1989) work was originally focused specifically on the experience of Black women, her work around intersectionality (see Cho, Crenshaw, and McCall 2013) has helped shape how we can understand the vast interactions and intersections of identities, such as sexualities, over time and across the world. Attwood (2018) says "[a] move towards intersectional feminist approaches has made it possible to think about the differences in women's experiences and priorities around the world, and to consider the ways that gender intersects with sexuality, race, ethnicity, and other aspects of identity" (23). Returning to Rosemarie Garland-Thomson's (2009) ideas on staring seems well suited to a discussion on our bodies as intersectional sexualized spaces and places. She states that, "while social rules script staring, individual improvisation can take the staring encounter in fruitful directions. Staring, in other words, makes things happen between people" (33). Her use of the word "fruitful" here feels as though a story should follow where people meet and a mutual exchange of information, even education, may transpire. Unfortunately, the "fruitful" story that is shared here is based on racism and sexualization.

Kali: So, I get harassed a lot in Ubers. Getting harassed or assaulted—as I have been—on a street is one thing, but being in the private yet public space of an Uber ride is another. I was getting harassed so often and it wasn't even just when I'm taking them, like, to go to work at the strip club, which would make it worse sometimes, but like, even any hours of the day, it would be like, they'd see my [real] name, which is an unusual name, but also can mean certain things in certain cultures, like, be significant in Middle Eastern cultures or any other Southeast Asian country. And, so, I get questions. The driver would be like, "Oh, where are you from?" A lot of times it would be well-meaning because the person was trying to connect based on a shared culture. But also, it was kind of too close, because people would be like, hitting on me or being hypersexualized with me as well. So, I say things like: "I'm just trying to get to a destination, trying to stay safe and this just makes me uncomfortable." And obviously, I don't need to disclose this because this is a service that is happening. So, this puts me in a weird sort of microaggression as it is now escalating into sexual harassment. All of this to say, this has happened a lot based on my name and my locations where they are bringing me. And then I ended up changing my name on Uber, to Ashley. I changed it to Ashley and my real last name because my father is Irish, and it is, like, a nice, quote–unquote "easy" name. My Uber rating for doing that has gone up by 0.5 points. That's actually a lot, and went from, like, a 4.8 to a 4.9. I had a lower rating before because I would talk back, or maybe [they would] give me lower ratings when it became clear that my race and sexuality wasn't a bargaining chip.

There are many intersectional elements working together here: safety, harassment, microaggressions, entitlement, "ethnic" names, public space, private space, and well-meaning strangers, amongst others. Body stories like Kali's expose the complexity of identities and experiences and demonstrate how these intersections lead to how people experience social privilege *and* systemic inequality every day of our lives. Consider how you have experienced interactions in public that have made you uncomfortable to the point of lying to strangers. What caused those feelings? How did you navigate them?

SEXUALIZATION, FETISHIZATION, AND EXOTICISM

Sexualization is a term that is used quite commonly, but it is has various meanings. Attwood (2018) says: "The term has been used to indicate how visible sex has become in contemporary culture, how preoccupied we are with sexual values and practices, [and] how new forms of sexual experience have emerged" (62). In Attwood's examples, she references how children are often exposed to sexualized imagery in the media and the various potentially negative consequences based on that exposure. Where can we see this? Toy catalogues. Music videos. Disney movies. When we consider sexualization, we must think of the ways it is gendered. Many young women are caught in a double-bind where any engagement with sexuality is seen to position them as a "slut," or if their sexual identities are not obvious enough, then they are prudish. As a sex worker, Kali's experience with sexualization is more overt than most women's as her sexuality is embedded in her job. Her experiences of sexualization, however, consistently intersect with male privilege, white supremacy, and power.

Kali: The racism that we experience out in the world gets really exacerbated in [the strip club]. The anti-Black racism in strip clubs is absolutely terrible. You can go online on Instagram and read horror stories about Black dancers being told you can't work in certain clubs or "we can't have more than three Black girls on the floor" and toxic, like, stuff like that. And in the club, it was very raw. I had a customer one time say, "What's your background? Oh, you're half white and half Brown. Well, maybe you can scrub your dirty brown skin a little harder so we see more of the white." Somebody just straight up said that to me. But they pay money … maybe to see naked girls, and knowing that we don't actually get part of that cover fee first of all. And then they come in to rip on the girls and to just talk shit to us. And that is a complicated space to occupy, because I will take this money back from the patriarchy. I will take it back from racists. One time I gave a lap dance to a Donald Trump supporter who was wearing a Make America Great Again hat. He was totally racist but wanted a dance from me because it was a weird fucked-up fetish that he had. I was like, "Well, I'm gonna take this money because these are my reparations. Yeah, I'll take the money from the racist and pay my bills with it!" It's that same balance again of feeling vulnerable, but also being empowered because I understand the systems and, you know, when that person says, "Scrub your dirty brown skin," or, "Oh, I don't want you, I want a white blonde girl," or, "I love Donald Trump, but dance for me, exotic brown piece of shit" … it's certainly affected me. It was vivid.

The ways that Kali is discussing her experiences of sexism and racism are deeply rooted in patriarchal understandings of the sexualized and racialized bodies of women. **Patriarchy** can be defined as a system of societal oppression where men and masculinity hold dominant positions of power and influence, specifically in terms of political and social institutions. Bryan S. Turner (1984) claims that "any sociology of the body involves a discussion of social control and any discussion of social control must consider the control of women's bodies by men under a system of patriarchy" (3). Here, Turner is explaining how the historically unchallenged discourses of patriarchy—which provide the framework for much of our social existence—have impacted our understandings of bodies and their social significances. Turner references the work of feminist theorists as he implies that the study of the body in society must be found within the analysis of female subordination in different forms of patriarchal relations. However, "[t]o say that patriarchal relations are structural is to suggest that they exist in the institutions and social practices of our society and cannot be explained by the intentions, good or bad, of individual women or men" (Weedon 1987, 3). When we critically examine these patriarchal social practices, such as how sexist beliefs inform notions of masculine privilege, then we are able to contextualize experiences and analyze social power. For example, in the above quote, Kali uses the word "patriarchy" to describe the violent, racist, sexualization by men in the strip club, which is comparable to the ways that

Alice describes how she comes to expect the fetishization of her trans body because of strict patriarchal beliefs about gendered presentations.

Alice: I have been a trans fetish even before I was trans. I mean, I was always trans, but I came out at 21, so before that people were telling me that I looked like a girl and wanted to dress me up and make me into their pretty little ... whatever. I have always considered being someone else's fetish as part of my existence. It's not even tied to my gender at this point. It's just tied to how I look and how I present. So that's me—I'm an interesting conundrum.

Kali and Alice both experience the fetishization of their gendered appearances and sexuality. To be **fetishized** is an active process of being positioned as a sexualized object of desire, intrigue, or worship. For fetishization to take place, explicit sexual engagements or encounters do not need to be happening—fetishization can happen based on a wide array of witnessed appearances and behaviours. As Alice describes above, her very existence within a trans body encourages a sexualization that positions her as a fetish object. Similarly, Kali's experience takes on a racialized dimension in her fetishized encounters where her brown femme body is read through racist framings of her being somehow **exotic**, meaning wild and foreign.

Recall from Kali's body story that Uber drivers (amongst others) often ask her the fairly common question of "where are you from?" Gillian Creese (2019) claims that this question is pervasive in Canadian society and is aimed toward those who do not fit the image of "a Canadian," which is as racist as it sounds. "For those who are born in or mostly raised in Canada, routine queries about 'where are you from' suggest that although their bodies convey local attributes, nevertheless, they are perceived to be from somewhere else and are called upon to account for their presence by identifying other origins" (Creese 2019, 1476). This racist expectation of racialized people being from somewhere else is also closely connected to a presumed sexualized exoticness due to their origin being mystical and unknown.

Ulrike Schaper et al. (2020) discuss a concept that might help illuminate this, which they have termed "sexotic." As they note below, the term **sexotic** helps to conceptualize why and how sexual interest in the Other is still so pervasive throughout Western culture.

> We place special emphasis on processes of sexualization that construct the "exotic" as sexually attractive, desirable and stimulating. This dimension of sexoticization entails, for example, the sexual fetishization of a certain skin color or images of the beach as a space that facilitates passionate sex. The term sexotic thus serves to expose the sexual quality commonly associated with the exotic and the exotic quality associated with sex. We understand the sexotic as a strictly relational category that is applied to express the polyvalent relation towards places, people, objects and practices that marks them as fascinating and desirable yet simultaneously different and often threatening. (115–16)

Here, we can see the intersectional ways that the histories and stigmas of Other bodies intersect within discourses of sexoticism. It is through movement and the results of European imperialism, Schaper et al. (2020) argue, that these sexotic practices flourish. This is because European imperialism gave direct political significance to the primacy of masculinity and whiteness and, thus, has helped to establish, justify, and maintain sexist and racist relations of power around the world.

This reality of fetishization and exoticism does not diminish Kali and Alice, however. As noted in Kali's statement above: "I was like, 'Well, I'm gonna take this money because these are my reparations. Yeah, I'll take the money from the racist and pay my bills with it!'" This is a powerful commentary on Kali's active and fierce resistance to the dominant narratives that she lives within as she discusses how the use of her money from stripping helped her to pay her way through higher education. While some might say that it is her choice to engage in sex work and she should live with the consequences, everyone deserves to live in a space where they can engage in sexual play and employment without fear of racist and sexualized violence. Similarly, Alice describes the way that she responds to people when they ask invasive questions with the goal of educating them: "I just hope that the things that I do with my body and the things that I say in general will maybe help people realize the errors in what they're doing when they come up to me. I want to make them question their questions. I also want to use my online platform to educate. Ideally, I would love to do a lecture series." It is clear from both of these anecdotes that both Kali and Alice desire to use their embodied experiences to educate themselves and others about the fluid nature of gender, performance, and the very closed-minded categories that they are often boxed within.

SEX CRITICAL

Alice and Kali demonstrate the various ways you can speak back to the dominant culture when it is assuming too much regarding your sexuality. Here, we can explore what it means to be **sex critical**. Attwood (2018) defines the ability to be sex critical as one that does not rely solely on the idea that we must be sex positive or sex negative, but rather we must think critically and question how the notion of "sexuality" impacts the ways we experience ourselves and others. The basis for framing one's approach to sexuality as neither wholly positive nor negative is a rather new idea.

Lisa Downing (2012) seemingly coined the term "sex critical" through her criticism of the feminist response to the *Fifty Shades of Grey* trilogy by E. L. James (2011). Downing states:

> On the one hand, liberal or "sex-positive" feminists and activists criticized the book's gender stereotyping and the (in)accuracy of its portrayal of BDSM, but defended strongly its exploration of sexual practices and behaviours and promoted the beneficent effects on female readers of exposure to erotic material—any erotic material. On the other hand, certain members of the radical feminist, anti-BDSM fringe used *Fifty Shades* as something of a pretext for furthering an agenda which holds that there is no difference between BDSM and domestic abuse, both being versions of the heteronormative patriarchal archiplot. (n.p.)

Downing (2012) is arguing that we don't have to have a wholly positive or negative response to the book—or what the bodies are doing in the book—for our response to be a feminist one. Being sex-positive does not negate how we can critique sexual representations that may be both empowering and stereotypical, or worse. Downing explains a few aspects of what it means to be sex critical:

- All forms of sexuality and all sexual representations should be equally susceptible to critical thinking and interrogation about the normative or otherwise ideologies they uphold.
- The discursive trappings of heterosexual relationships, intercourse, and reproduction deserve just as much critical scrutiny as non-normative identities/behaviours/presentations and "extreme" bodily practices (if not more, given the historical lack of critical attention brought to bear on what is perceived to be the norm, leading to unquestioning acceptance of potential inequalities and harm). (n.p.)

Alice summarizes a sex critical framework when discussing her relationships to femininity and the sexualized presentation of self. She states, "I'm almost used to my body being seen as a spectacle at this point. This sounds kind of saddening, but maybe also empowering? Whatever your gender is, if you present in a way that is typically more feminine, people will automatically take that as an invitation. The invitation could be sexual, staring, questions, whatever. It is the femininity that creates it. I find that interesting." To be sex critical does not deny the painful experiences of fetishization and exoticism. As Elizabeth Grosz (1994) states, "[i]t is the ability of bodies to always extend the frameworks which attempt to contain them, to seep beyond their domains of control" (xi). All of the participants in this book have bodies that push the boundaries of comfort for those around them. It is through their persistence in existing in a world that wants to disempower them that reparations and education can begin to take shape, as evidenced by the strength of Kali and Alice's voices.

KEY WORDS

Exotic; Fetishized; Heteronormative; Homonormative; Patriarchy; Sex; Sex critical; Sex positive; Sexotic; Sexuality; Sexualization

QUESTIONS FOR REFLECTION AND DISCUSSION

1. If you had to define the ways that gender, sex, and sexuality are distinct but related, what would you say?

2. Alice says that she is used to her body being a spectacle, and that "this sounds kind of saddening, but also empowering." What do you think this means? How can the ways that our bodies appear be saddening and empowering simultaneously?

3. Look again at the way that Kali and Alice were visually interpreted by Damian. What do you think could have been added or removed? Why?

Underestimated and Overdetermined: Shame, Tokenism, Exoticism, and Fierce Resistance

Body Story: Viola

In moments, I'm exhausted. Like, it's midnight and I just want to say to this random person messaging me for help with their homework: "Can I be your token Native acquaintance tomorrow?"

—Viola

Viola may be soft-spoken, but her words are very powerful. Our interview was one that flowed comfortably and, yet, was full of quiet pauses of intentional reflection. At 24, Viola is in graduate school, exploring questions of Indigeneity and gender in higher education. Viola describes herself as both quiet and chatty, annoying and thoughtful, caring, positive, and open-minded. If she were a cartoon character, she thinks she would be Bubbles from *The Powerpuff Girls*. As an Indigenous woman living in Northern Ontario, she fields questions from strangers on a regular basis, mostly stemming from her skin colour.

Viola: I get the "so, what are you?" all the time. I am not even joking. I have been asked that question hundreds of times, hundreds of times, hundreds of times. I went to an all-French elementary school and I think that I was the darkest person at that school. So, I just remember people pointing out my difference because I was darker than everyone else. My hair was dark and curly. The experience was full of microaggressions. "Why are you so tan? What's wrong with your hair?" It was a lot.

Viola has a love of all things feminine. While she describes her personal style as somewhat plain, she expresses joy at a discussion of make-up and beauty products. Viola goes on to describe how she has complex relationships with her hair, similar to the other body stories in this book. She also expresses how, in public, she has been tokenized, disrespected, and experienced racist vitriol, but she still believes that, inherently, most people are well-meaning strangers. She says, "I don't think questions often come from a mean place ... probably an ignorant place. Actually,

I think it comes from a place of curiosity, but that's not an excuse for ignorance either." There were many moments where Viola was reflecting aloud during our interview and her thoughts would change or become more nuanced as the conversation went on. To me, it was an exhilarating conversation because it showed the depth of Viola's experiences and her ability to articulate them while recognizing it as a process—a journey of discovery, clarity, and safety.

Viola describes an experience where the "what are you" question took on significant meaning for her.

Viola: There was this one time, with my ex-boyfriend, where we went to a get-together with a bunch of his family—all white people. And there was this one person, staring at me from across the table. She was just staring. I was just not really sure what to do, so I just tried not to make eye contact with her. Then, out of nowhere, she just bursts out and asks me, "So, what are you?" I couldn't even believe that it happened. The table went quiet. Who asks that? I mean, I know who. But I still can't believe it when it happens. I remember that I said, "Oh, I'm a student!" to try to deflect it. She wasn't listening to the conversation around her. I'm not even sure she heard my answer. She was so fixated on the "whys" in her head: Why is she different? Why does she look like that? I'm an Indigenous woman, but that makes me different than other racialized people. There are a lot of different characterizations for me.

It was this experience that Viola returned to on a number of occasions in our interview. It became emblematic of the experiences that she has in public and private spaces—about who she is, why she is here, and what it is that people may want from her.

Interestingly, in our interview, Viola would alternate between referring to herself as Indigenous and Native. *Native* is another collective term (see our discussion of *Indigenous* in Chapter 1), which speaks to the ways that Viola navigates the impact that colonization has had and continues to have. Viola embodies a complex duality. For example, this duality was demonstrated through her fear to speak back to those who hurl racism toward her—as demonstrated in her deflection in the dinner party scene—and how this is contrasted by her lack of fear when she embodies her role as Indigenous feminist activist. Viola even said, at one point: "I don't ever defend myself, but for other people? I am willing to do anything. Say anything. No fear." Perhaps it is Viola's shyness that gives the appearance of this duality, but I think that there is something more to be said about the in-between, which we will explore in this chapter.

Viola
Damian Mellin, 2020

Within Viola's transcript, it was hard to pin down what she was like. A large focus of the conversation fell on how other people treated her and her reactions to them. Within the illustration, I wanted to give all the white people around her a sense of blandness in contrast to her strength. Using a plain yogurt container as inspiration, I illustrated the white, male characters in bland vibe so that she could shine through.—Damian Mellin

Body Story: Gioia

*Depending on my mood and if I'm feeling more or less charitable, I will
be similarly more or less polite or pleasant in my reaction to whatever
comment is thrown my way. But it definitely annoys me when it impedes
with my general experience of being a person in the world.*

—Gioia

If my interview with Viola can be described as quiet with many intentional pauses, my interview with Gioia can best be described as the exact opposite. I spoke little; Gioia spoke quickly, passionately, and with unparalleled linguistic gymnastics about her embodied existence. In her role as a university professor, she has lived in a variety of major cities in Canada, but, at 40, Gioia finds herself living on the East Coast. Her body story has two different flavours, as she says.

Gioia: So first, I either get the talking about my appearance in a "What's your ethnicity? You look very exotic" kind of way, which I still tend to see as to be sort of commenting on my body. And so people are people willing to comment on my looks and be like, "Oh, you look so exotic," or like, "Where are you from?" And so I get that a lot, especially out here. I find that I sort of read in any context as the most accessible ethnic population that there is. So, here, people think I'm Lebanese a lot.

The other flavour is about my shape. I am a very curvy woman. I think some days I feel like I have comically large breasts. I have a booty ... like, a real booty. I thankfully still have a bit of a waist. So, like, I come in on an hourglass halfway. And so I mean, don't get me wrong, I definitely know where I do my best work and I play that up accordingly in different situations when I dress, but my breasts are sort of the most noticeable feature from my neck down. For my whole life, that's been sort of, like, a thing that I've had to contend with.

Gioia's body story encapsulates a variety of themes already covered, but in markedly different ways. Gioia may be misracialized as a woman of colour because she has a darker skin tone, but she is white. So, her experience of these racialized encounters does not have the same effect on her because her identity as Italian disrupts the narrative if it is disclosed (which will be discussed in this chapter). She is sexualized—as all women are—but the sexualization that she receives is primarily and specifically connected to the size of her breasts. These experiences lead Gioia to describe her encounters with strangers as coming from both places of curiosity to places of abject sexism and racism. For her, these encounters are also constant. She describes sexualized surveillance, fetishization online and offline, and a continual self-monitoring of how she presents. In one of her stories, she discloses a scene that encapsulates what must have been a non-event for a stranger and a terrifying ordeal for Gioia.

Gioia: I was on a party boat cruise with some friends. And this guy saw me and came up to me and he was just kind of appraising my boobs and kept looking at me up and down. Like, who just comes up to somebody to stare them up and down and, you know, look at them straight in the nipple line, right? And he looks at me and says, "Hello, I … like … your … *shaaaape.*" His voice was monotone and flat. And I said "Okay? Thank you." And in my mind, I was like, cool, cool, great, okay, bye. And I just spent the whole rest of the party boat avoiding him. He was constantly looking for me to talk to me. One of my friends was there and he thought this was hilarious and I just finally lost it and I was like, "This isn't funny. He's bothering me, like, I just want to have fun with you guys. I'm not here to be harassed by some dude who, like, is gonna stare me up and down with, like, a devious look in his eye." Then he says again, but way more slowly, almost like a hiss: "I … like … your … shape." Yeah, really, dude? How about you ask me my fucking name? So, the boat cruise ended and I was like, "Guys, I will see you at the car." I have the car keys and so I bolted to the car and I got inside. I was so freaked out, Victoria. I was leaning the seat—the driver's seat—flat back so that no one would see me. And thankfully the windows were tinted, and I could see him. He was still looking to see if he could spot me in the crowd. It was so creepy. I am a person and I'm a person with feelings. And, you know, I appreciate that men can have specific interests of body parts, but like, I have a name and I have interests and I have likes and dislikes. And I have good days and I have bad days and I have hobbies and I have a career and I struggle. I'm, like, a whole person. I would like to be seen as a whole person beyond breasts.

I have included this story here not because it encompasses who Gioia is, but because it gives a glimpse into what she carries with her. This is just one story that she told me less than five minutes into our hour-long conversation. It was wedged between a story about a woman—who Gioia believes likely lives with mental illness—pointing to Gioia while she was working at a bank and loudly exclaiming: "You have the hugest tits I have ever seen!" The story that followed was regarding a man who she dated who did not fixate on her breasts and how this was so unusual for her that it was almost shocking.

Gioia
Damian Mellin, 2020

This was the hardest drawing for me to produce. So many male artists gravitate to large-breasted women in their anime comic art life that it's something I have avoided in my art illustrations. I was extremely heartbroken to hear about how she had gone to have this amazing adventure only to be put in a spot where she was hiding in a blazing hot car. The influence from this story formed this hypercoloured image inspired by Grand Theft Auto. *For load screens, they use these illustrations of objectified women in swimsuits. I wanted to reclaim those graphics to show a woman, living and feeling something.*—Damian Mellin

Body Theories: Responding to Viola and Gioia

LIVING IN THE BETWEEN

This chapter has been the most challenging for me to write. Viola and Gioia have offered so many topics to engage with that it has been difficult to figure out how to capture them without also diminishing them. Viola has experienced many elements of embodiment that we have only scratched the surface of in this book: racialization, dehumanization, and exoticization. Similarly, Gioia has also experienced many crossovers with other body stories: sexualization, exoticization, racialization, and privilege. Having said this, for both Viola and Gioia, through their body stories, they convey a duality far stronger than in others. They speak to a sense of being in-between, stuck, proud of who they are, but navigating the complexities of the expectations and assumptions around them. They are both misidentified continually. Both are strong, yet recognize that to retreat to safety does not diminish them. Their stories express grappling with feelings of being underestimated and **overdetermined**. To be overdetermined refers to how we account for or create meaning for something due to multiple causes or with more conditions than are necessary. This means that we, as a society, tend to ascribe more meaning onto certain identities and base those meanings on variables that could be completely unrelated; this is particularly true in terms of racialized meanings. As a result, this chapter will speak to some of the complexities of being shamed for your identity and body, experiences of passing, tokenism, and exoticization (racially and sexually). Lastly, and perhaps most importantly, this chapter will explore how Viola and Gioia are both fierce resistors of the narratives that are thrust upon them.

BEING SHAMED AND UNDERESTIMATED

In every body story I have ever heard, there is **shame**. In conversation with one of my best friends who is also a therapist, she refers to shame as the "nuclear bomb of emotion" because it is the hardest emotion to name, acknowledge, and wrestle with and once you do acknowledge it, there is no going back. Shame is a well-developed mechanism of control for women in order to discipline their bodies so as to force them to (attempt to) meet cultural ideals (Orenstein 2016). Shame is also about visibility. "When one experiences shame, one is seen (by oneself or others) to be doing something untoward or inappropriate" (Dolezal 2015, xv). Shame is a "self-feeling that is felt by and on the body," as Sara Ahmed (2004, 103) notes. Jessica Ringrose and Laura Harvey (2015) argue that body shaming and "slut shaming" have historically been an integral component to the construction of sexuality as it relates to feminized bodies. Shame goes beyond the sexual, however. As Sheila Cote-Meek (2014) argues, "[m]uch to our dismay, there is no doubt that the bodies of Aboriginal peoples have been marked in very specific ways in order to maintain existing hierarchies that keep us locked in a particular space and place" (37). This marking that Cote-Meek refers to is an attempt to imprint shaming upon the bodies of Indigenous peoples, but the role of shame is more complex than this implies. Further, as Ahmed (2004) notes, "the very physicality of shame—how it works on and through bodies—means that shame also involves the de-forming and re-forming of bodily and social spaces" (103). Shame is an internalization of the socio-cultural feelings that circulate around certain bodies, and its function is to make it known to women of all ages and gendered presentations that they are always already in a relationship with shaming—either it has or it will happen.

Luna Dolezal (2015) writes extensively on the connections between the body and shame. She argues that shame is a cultural inheritance for women. As she notes, "[d]escribing not only the chronic shame of those who believe their bodies to be somehow defective or socially deficient, body shame also occurs in acute cases where during social interaction one's self presentation falters or fails. What is more often described as embarrassment shame, in this acute sense, is a mechanism of social control which ensures bodily order" (xvi). We can see these practices in hair straightening, covering of cleavage, avoidance of tight clothing, the application of make-up, cosmetic procedures, and so on. While there are complex webs of reasons that people desire to alter their bodies, a key argument could be made that many of these gendered practices serve to ensure a bodily order to avoid shame.

> Body shame, in short, can be understood to be shame that arises as a result of the body. It comes about as a result of some aspect of the body or bodily management, perhaps appearance, bodily functions or comportment. It is shame that is centred on the body, where the subject believes their body to be undesirable or unattractive, falling short of social depictions of the "normal," the ideal or the socially acceptable body. (Dolezal 2015, 7)

Again, it is through the power of the stare that these feelings of shame are initially felt through the body. "We say something to one another when we stare. Staring is part of our enormous communal vocabulary of the eyes that we use to put a sharp point on what we mean, think, or want" (Garland-Thomson 2009, 39). We take in that sharp point of the stranger and it matters to us what we believe the stare can mean. For example, one of the questions that I asked each participant was: "What is an assumption that people make of you?" The ways that we internalize the encounters we have had and the (verbal and non-verbal) disclosures that people make to us are compelling.

Nana: I think it is assumed that I am nice and non-threatening.

Rae: That I am open to being asked any question about my Blackness. Maybe it is also because I am short and a woman? I dunno.

Kali: Maybe that I'm hopeless? No, a lot less independent or self-sufficient than I actually am. Maybe they assume also more innocence—like diminutive, childlike too—possibly because of these giant eyeballs that I have. They see five foot one. These are things I think people assume of shorter women.

Alice: People currently assume that I'm very kind, sweet, and naive. And then, funnily enough, before I transitioned, people used to assume that I was very intimidating and frightening and deadpan. So that was kind of a total one-eighty. Partly because, you know, I actually smile now.

Viola: People think I am quiet and therefore I have nothing to say. They also think I am anything but Native; usually that I am Mexican or Black.

Gioia: That I am too much—too much of everything—to be a professor. I don't look like whatever prof is in their mind.

Quinn (whose body story follows this chapter): I think they don't think I'm as smart as I really am. That I am an airhead. I think that they think I am actually a lot nicer than not just—I really am nice—but I think people don't think that I can be assertive.

If I were to answer this question for myself, it would go something like this:

Victoria: I assume that people think I am attention-seeking, snobbish, over-the-top, and that the way my body looks must mean that I am not very bright. I am (or was) either sporty or a model.

These feelings are not shame*less* because most of them are expressed as a misreading, a misidentification, and/or something undesirable. As Dolezal (2015) says, "[a]lthough shame is a self-focused experience and does not necessarily entail concrete presence of others, it is inherently a social emotion and has an undeniably social dimension" (5). Many of these examples speak to the ways that the participants feel underestimated by those around them. I find them challenging to read because the connotations of niceness are lacking assertiveness, being too much, too little, never enough. From what I know of these women, it describes none of them and, yet, these are the things that they assume and feel reflected back about themselves from others. Consider for yourself: If I were to ask you, "What is an assumption that people make about you?," what would you say? As we move through the rest of the chapter, try to come up with your own answer.

Susie Orbach (2009) says, "We are judged physically and our social and economic position has depended on how our bodies are seen and where we are then placed socially and economically" (165). The above descriptions are the ways that we place ourselves in the minds of others, but those assumptions are not based on paranoia or a misguided sense of the negativity of others. They are based on the internalization of our bodies as somehow wrong.

Viola: Growing up, I never identified as Indigenous. I just felt a little embarrassed by it. There was just always so much stigma about Indigenous people being bums, and all these negative stereotypes ... I just didn't bother. I actually remember in one of my history classes, we had to build a 3D model of when settlers came to Canada and built farms on "seigneuries," which was land allocated to different families. I just felt really small during the whole project, it was an overall unsettling thing to work on. People would just assume I was Greek or Italian or what have you; I wouldn't agree or deny the assumptions. I'd just go with it.

Being shamed is a cultural process. Being shamed for one's identity is what Viola is expressing here. Is Viola ashamed of being Indigenous? As you know from her body story, Viola is a proud Indigenous woman, but this story reflects that it was a difficult journey through adolescence for her to discover that pride. As Cote-Meek (2014) discusses, "[s]adly, one way to resist ongoing colonialism and racism is to actually deny one's own identity. If one can distance oneself from labels and racialized constructions, a cushion against the daily barrage of attacks is formed" (128). As an Indigenous woman, Viola experiences racism and simultaneously experiences gendered oppression: "Gender differences raise particularly important issues. Indigenous women's ways of knowing are shaped by their livelihoods and shared experiences of racism, colonialism, and by their experiences as leaders, mothers, sisters, and grandmothers" (Altamirano-Jiménez and Kermoal 2016, 9). Racism and colonialism are embedded in Viola's experiences of her body. In her discussion of her hair, body shape, mannerisms, family, partner, schooling, and daily interactions, her gendered Indigeneity is filtered through racist assumptions embedded within discourses of nation and personhood as read upon her body. It reflects a false or double consciousness, a term that W. E. B. Du Bois named to describe when oppressed peoples look at themselves through the eyes of the privileged. As Shalene Jobin (2016) explains, "within this racially prejudiced world, black persons see themselves mistakenly, in the way that the white world sees them" (41). Jobin connects this double consciousness to Indigenous folks as well, saying that "resistance to assimilation and efforts to heal the double consciousness have occurred and continue to occur" (2016, 50). She sees this healing happening through telling the stories of Indigenous peoples as this affirms identities, lands, and being in the world in order to lay claim to these intergenerational traumas and silences.

As we can see throughout the above discussion, being shamed is a cultural process, as well as a social process. For Viola, shame functions so that she experiences oppression on a number of axes—gender and race, as well as class and age. This is most obvious as she describes the following encounter she had while working as a bartender at a baseball tournament.

Viola: I think I've just like gotten used to it [racism], which is kind of sad. But, it's because you never know what someone's gonna say. I remember once I was bartending, at a baseball tournament in [a small community], which is 45 minutes from here. And it's very French there. And I guess the man I served beer to didn't assume that I spoke French and he just said under his breath to his friends, in French, he said, "They've got savages serving us now?" [*long pause*] In my head I was like, "Oh my God, like, oh my God, that just happened." I couldn't even believe it.

In this situation, Viola did not say anything or give any indication that she understood what the man said. We talked about the colonial violence inherent in the word "savage," the unequal power dynamics between her, as a service worker, and the customer, the age difference, racial disparity, and the fear, shock, and trauma that she felt in that moment.

Dolezal's (2015) ideas are important here as well: "[G]reat efforts are made to control the female body and its behaviour through shaming strategies that have the twofold effect of disciplining women's bodies and also appointing the behaviours that are appropriate for them" (107). The ways in which Viola's body was being disciplined by the customer are akin to the ways Gioia describes her experiences of bodily shaming as well. If you remember from Gioia's body story, the persistent social encounters that she has regarding the size of her breasts provide her with daily reminders that her body is "too much." (We will further discuss excess in Chapter 5.) Is she ashamed of her breasts? No. Does she make choices to avoid shame? Yes.

Gioia: I have a huge whole, like, practice around professional dressing. And I actually gave a presentation to the Women's Studies first-year students about how I choose to dress the way I dress. One, because I'm young-ish for a prof and I look young and two, because I'm a woman. So, I make sure, for example, that on a teaching day, it's not like I have turtlenecks on but if I have to bend over, then I want to avoid a crazy amount of cleavage, right? I like to wear dresses and feel femme, but it's all strategic. So that it's not about looking at me as an object. It's about sort of me putting forward, like, a professional projection, right? Like, this is me, I am your prof. I'm here to teach you. And I take my job seriously, so I look nice, but like … it's a fine line to straddle and especially for me where, you know, literally anything that sort of gives me eight inches of neck gets cleavage.

I chose to include this story here even though it might seem like a stretch to say that Viola's experience of racism is in any way similar to Gioia's sexualization, but the ways in which they talk about their body management are similar. Viola discusses how she didn't respond to those men because she "feared their reaction," straightens her hair to avoid being read as Black, and describes her personal style as "very plain on the regular," even though she is "outgoing and really loud in moments." Gioia similarly describes how she loves her body, doesn't want to hide any aspect of herself, and isn't "there for the enjoyment of men," yet her story about her workplace wardrobe depicts the kind of embodied management that many women can relate to. These are the messy realities that shame structures for us.

PASSING

Body management can take on many forms, one of which is passing. In academic circles, **passing** is primarily written about through (at least) two distinct practices, the first being its (outdated) association of relating to a social deception or lie. Anna Camaiti Hostert (2007) argues that this traditional theoretical approach to passing positions the passer as "[o]ne [who] sees oneself in a certain way yet deceptively presents oneself in a manner contradictory to that vision. Passing is to present oneself as something that one is not; it is a matter of violating the laws of identity and sameness (12). The second, more nuanced approach to notions of passing positions the passer as someone who is involved in self-preservation or self-protection: "By passing, individuals travel through fluid, multifaceted phases of their existence, experiencing a multidimensional identity as a remedy against forms of indifference or hostility towards the other" (Camaiti Hostert 2007, 80). For our purposes, I am using the second description to address instances of a practice (which can be active or passive) of passing, such as remaining silent about a queer identity when it may be unsafe to "out" oneself or, in Viola's case, "just going with" how people perceived her racialization in high school. The first definition seems to haunt the second one, in that passing can seem both like a strategy/practice and a means through which to engage with feelings of shame, guilt, and anxiety about one's identities and body.

Passing is not a simple process. As Tanya Titchkosky (2003) argues, "[t]o be marginal and to pass as ordinary is to find one's self positioned somewhere between a set of expectations about what any 'normal' self ought to be and the actual work involved in these 'doings of ordinariness'" (69). Throughout our interviews, the participants who speak to moments where they "pass" primarily characterize it as a process. By this I mean that most of them did not announce "I pass in this way," but rather, stories of passing emerged casually and slowly throughout the telling of their body stories. For example, Alice describes her experiences of being read as masculine or feminine, as well as male or female, depending on the context. Viola also describes how often she passes as Lebanese, Mexican, or Black. Again, these instances seem largely context-dependent, and they are never expressed as something that any of the participants are particularly comfortable with. This could be because "[p]assing never feels natural. It is a second skin that never adheres" (Kroeger 2003, 8). Brooke Kroeger is arguing here that the act of passing implies a sense of discomfort. Viola's internalization of a cultural and racialized history that she feels both a part of and also historically disconnected from becomes a messy reality for her when she passes as non-Indigenous.

For Gioia, her ambiguous skin tone sparks many questions from strangers, mostly because she passes as non-white.

Gioia: "Oh, you look so exotic!" or like, "Where are you from?" And so I get that a lot, especially out on the East Coast. ... So, here, people think I'm Lebanese a lot. ... I mean, I don't have any feelings about being read as Lebanese because, yeah, I appreciate that. People are trying to locate me socially. But it's always funny to see what people think I am and then people are always like, "Oh, you look so exotic." And I'm ... "So, what does that mean? What do you think I look like?" And then it's, "Oh, you know, you look Lebanese. Are you Lebanese?" Or, you know, "Are you Persian?" or whatever it happens to be, and often it's what they are or what someone close to them is and then I sort of look accessible in that way.

Gioia describes how this goes on for a while as she does not disclose to them "what she is" because she wants to educate and engage.

Gioia: They usually get to a point where they can tell I am playing with them and then they say something to the effect of, "I don't want to insult you." So, I reply: "If you didn't want to insult me, you should have never asked this question. Because it doesn't matter what my race or ethnicity is." I think more it's an attempt to either make conversation or break the ice or find some sort of familiarity or commonality with me. When I tell people I'm Italian then, the exotic comments flow. And I'm like, "Well, it's not really that exotic. It's like one of the biggest ethnic communities in Canada. So ..."

To pass as the Other is often a unique situation. More often than not, people pass as "normal" and reap the rewards that come along with privileged normality. As Erving Goffman (1963) notes, "[b]ecause of the great rewards in being considered normal, almost all persons who are in a position to pass will do so on some occasion by intent" (74).

Goffman's claim here also points to how the desire to pass is not only for those who want to pass as privileged, but also for those who want to pass in order to be included. For Gioia, passing as Other seemingly reflects her inability to "do whiteness right." Here, her "exotic" body—as over-sexualized and ambiguously racialized—intersects to speak to her inability to often pass as normal.

Perhaps we can see the in-between spaces that Viola and Gioia occupy to reflect their inability to nicely or easily fit into dominant narratives that attempt to confine them: "Passing, then, is a way of evading the increasingly categorical imperative of belonging, of affiliation, which attaches labels to everybody, assigning roles that soon turn out to be cages" (Camaiti Hostert 2007, 80). This connection between belonging and passing is something that is key to consider. For example, in "La Conciencia de la Mestiza: Towards a New Consciousness," Gloria Anzaldúa (2001) describes the "cultural collision" of bodies and identities that occurs through transnationality: "The coming together of two self-consistent but habitually incompatible frames of reference causes un choque, a cultural collision" (766). This idea of a collision of cultures can be easily applied to the collision of bodies, of identities. Those who identify in the spaces between—multiracial people, visibly non-disabled, bi/trans/queer people—confirm the very idea that privileged identities, such as whiteness and masculinity, are not fixed or absolute. The privileges that accompany these identities are also dependent upon the space that they are in and how they are interpreted, which can shift depending upon the space a body is occupying/sharing.

As Minelle Mahtani (2001) states in her discussion of embodying a multiethnic identity, "not all multiethnic women have the freedom to identify as multiethnic. Strict rules about the politics of categorisation often makes this impossible" (184–85). While it may be that identities are always partial, or "not quite" what they appear, these in-between moments are often ignored in order for us to make easy judgements about one another. Further, in their discussion of multiracial identities, David Parker and Miri Song (2001) suggest that "falling in-between these socially constructed norms leaves one open to statements which doubt corporeal integrity: 'You don't look Chinese ...' on a par with

'You don't look quite *right*'" (14). Problematically, not looking "right" often results in positioning a body as "exotic," which also relies on the ways that racial classifications are malleable and so often positions racialized peoples as racially inferior. For Viola, she names this particularly in terms of dating apps: "When I have been dating online, exotic comes up over and over. My worth is strictly something exotic for white guys to go out with or whatever, because I am Native or I look Other to you." This type of exoticism is characterized by the intersection of being non-white and subsequently being assumed to be hypersexual and untouched by Canadianness. This foreignness then provides an intimate interest for a spectator who has been taught to desire bodies meant for white men to conquer and sexually experience (Waring 2013).

TOKENIZED AND EXOTICIZED

Tokenism is the process whereby people of various identities are made to stand in as the singular person or limited group of people with knowledge and expertise in order to provide legitimacy. Tokens are expected to share their subjective knowledge on behalf of whatever identity the dominant group wants to know more about, and they are often not valued for their ideas on any issues that do not relate to the identity that is being tokenized (Cote-Meek 2014).

In sharing the body stories of the participants, my goal has never been for them to be made into caricatures of whatever identity we are discussing, but rather showing that they are whole people with journeys and stories that change over the course of their lives. It is a challenging line to straddle. As Elizabeth Grosz (1994) notes, "[t]he body is a most peculiar 'thing,' for it is never quite reducible to being merely a thing; nor does it ever quite manage to rise above the status of thing. Thus it is both a thing and a nonthing, an object, but an object which somehow contains or coexists with an interiority, an object able to take itself and others as subjects, a unique kind of object not reducible to other objects" (xi). In certain spaces and places of society, people are asked to "step in" and speak on behalf of entire groups of people—either with their words or even just the placement of their bodies. For Viola, this happens when she is the one Indigenous person seemingly used for a photo opportunity to demonstrate diversity in her institution.

Viola: I'm very tokenized. Especially when I was involved with, like, the Board of Governors of the university. I would see barely any women, or women of colour, on any of the university's boards. So, I just felt awkward all the time. And, there's always, like, these photo ops and then there's me and once again I am thinking to myself, "Oh my God, I'm the darkest person in every single photo" … there is such a lack of representation of women, but particularly racialized women, Indigenous women, in the university.

As Viola is expressing here, racialized bodies often become overdetermined. In her example above, she is standing in a photo because she feels that her skin colour (specifically) is being used to represent the supposed diversity of an academic institution. Viola's racialized body becomes an overdetermined symbol of inclusion, intersectionality, and the progressiveness of those standing with and around her—as if they can absorb these things through her presence. She notes this Othering and tokenization directly.

Providing evidence of difference within photographs is not a new phenomenon, of course. As we will explore at length in Chapter 5, the connection between our cultural characterizations and classifications of odd bodies and the history of the "freak show" is undeniable. Positioning extraordinary bodies as spectacles to consume in order to reestablish normality for the dominant group was once an acceptable common practice. As Robert Bogdan (1988) argues, the history of the "exotic presentation" in freak shows is now commonly known. The creation of the exotic Other was borne out of the European explorers' desire to position white colonialists as desirable humans and those from the non-Western world as savage wonders and scientific "missing links" that could provide evolutionary evidence of white "civilized" superiority. While I am always hesitant to provide a dictionary definition of a term, I think Merriam-Webster's definition of "exotic" is important to consider here. They define exotic as something "introduced from another country: not native to the place where found" and as "strikingly, excitingly, or mysteriously different or unusual," as well as "of or relating to striptease" (Merriam-Webster 2020). To summarize, in terms of a popular dictionary definition, something exotic is associated with difference, appearance, and sexual connotations.

For Gioia, her sexuality is exoticized using her breasts as the conduit. As Garland-Thomson (2009) notes, breasts are women's erotic capital. She says: "The visual magnetism of breasts can make both starers and starees anxious. Women often feel self-conscious about their breasted appearance. Too much breast means too much femininity; too little means not enough" (143). Gioia speaks to this characterization when she says: "It would be nice to have someone look me in the face and think that I'm pretty. Eye contact is not something I am super used to." She expressed that she has created some distance between herself and her breasts because of the way that they are so often framed as not for her, but for the pleasure of others. Being too feminine, too much, too objectified by her breasts and the size of her body is something Gioia describes as a fairly constant positioning she receives.

Living within the realm of the exotic comes with it a specific relationship to beauty norms that both Viola and Gioia express. Interestingly, they both discussed their experiences of online dating and reiterated a similar phrase that they receive:

Viola: People would say to me, "You're so pretty for a Native." There is this weird understanding that I am pretty in spite of being Native. So gross.

Gioia: They say, "You have such a pretty face." The subtext being, if I was thinner, then I would be pretty everywhere, but because I'm not, it's my face that is pretty. But also, like, it is almost a surprise.

Viola and Gioia were not the only two participants who had experiences like this, of course. Kali, Rae, and Alice also expressed similar instances of "You're so pretty for a ..." and you can fill in the blank with whatever seems objectifying enough. These are stigmatizing moments: "Stigmatizing is a social process that hurdles a body from the safe shadows of ordinariness into the bull's-eye of judgment" (Garland-Thomson

2009, 45). There exists a clash here where the participants are deftly aware of the limitations placed upon them, but also that these unequal and problematic structures of beauty and desire require us to give our bodies "constant attention" (Orbach 2009). Women often see these contradictions and fight internally to resist them. It is to this idea of resistance that we now turn.

RESISTANCE

Resistance is yet another complex idea. **Resistance** can mean to immediately refuse to accept or comply with something, but it can also mean to bear witness to something, to react passively and have that experience potentially spark future decision-making and social change (Mack and Na'puti 2019). In the subtitle for this book, I refer to "fierce resistance," but not because resistance is necessarily angry or aggressive; rather, I am using the term in the more contemporary usage that I am most familiar with. For example, on *RuPaul's Drag Race* (2009–Present) and in contemporary culture in general, if someone is fierce it means that they possess a great, intense, satisfying, powerful, and/or beautiful quality to them. If they are employing this fierceness in how they resist the public scrutiny around them, it can manifest in unexpected forms— subtly, loudly, and all meaningful. This use of language also exposes how resistance can be embodied diversely and has already been done so in the body stories that you have read thus far.

Feminized bodies are constantly under regulation and surveillance for how they exist in public. The normality and constancy of "beautiful" expectations are unrelenting and, ultimately, insidious and damaging. However, this does not mean that resistance is futile. Eli Clare (2009) frames the body as home, "but only if it is understood that bodies are never singular, but rather haunted, strengthened, underscored by countless other bodies" (11). It is through relationships with each other that we learn to resist that which tries to undermine us. In this concluding section, Viola and Gioia articulate their forms of resistance, primarily in their own words.

Viola: Years ago, I was watching my ex-boyfriend in a high school hockey game, and I was sitting with one of his teammates who wasn't playing [because] he was hurt. So, I was sitting with him and he was, like, chirping one of the players on the ice.

VK: I don't know what chirping is? Like yelling?

Viola: Yeah, like masculine commenting. Ha. ... And then the player on ice turns around and does, like, that hand movement over your mouth. I don't know what to call that, but to mock traditional Indians. And I just, I just stood there. And I was like, thinking, like, did that just happen? So, the period ended the hockey game, and I followed that team into their dressing room. I just followed them. And I just, I just lost it. I just had a total adrenaline rush and I just lost it. I was yelling because this guy did this racist gesture at us. I eventually got kicked out by security. Before that though, I said, "This is the most racist fucking thing I've ever seen in my life." And then the guy says, "Well, no, I wasn't doing that because he is Native. I did that because he's fat." I wasn't going to take that either so I pointed out then that's fat shaming someone. It's just as bad. I just lost it. And then, yeah, I had to get out of the dressing room. But moms from our team were like, "Oh, my God, like, that's awesome. As if you went and did that!" Well, no one else was, so someone had to. But I just was pumped. I was just like, oh my God. I do choose my battles, though, as you know; comments towards me personally ... I get quiet. Not this time.

Resistance comes in many forms. Confrontations are one form, but institutional activism is another.

Viola: Well, even a couple of years ago, I was on the committee to write sexual violence policy and one meeting they invited all the student leaders to meet up and go over it and I was the only woman in the room. Again, I actually lost it as I couldn't believe it was happening. A sexual violence policy meeting and I was the only woman. So, then I just called my own meeting and invited all the women and people from the pride committee. I wanted us to discuss: Why aren't we represented? It was disgusting. It was all male administrators too in the room. I just kept thinking to myself that these people are not gonna be able to write this policy and this policy won't matter ... I needed to start a new conversation.

Similarly, Gioia reflects on all of the time she has spent not resisting the discourses around her and now realizing how limiting that has been.

Gioia: Maybe the other thing that I'm really sort of weirdly starting to realize at 40 is that media narratives around what's sexy and what is sexually valued and even worth objectifying are, sort of, pretty flat. It's one note, right? It's like a butt and boobs and tiny waist but you also have to be a size four. All this weird shit that maybe three people in the world have. I recognize these things now in a way I never did before. I mean, I'm also a social scientist, but that doesn't mean I could really ever frame it for myself … until now.

It is in relation to those discourses that Gioia has decided to become empowered in embodied ways.

Gioia: As I have mentioned, my body is either hypersexualized or medicalized (a.k.a. I'm too fat). I don't want to connect this too much, but four to five times a week, more or less, I have started going to a gym. For me, working out is really sort of stress-busting and community building. This isn't a thinness project. The gym that I belong to right now is having what they call a transformation challenge. It's not a weight loss challenge; transformation challenge, though, fundamentally, the metric is weight loss, whenever. So, I love this gym, and I've never said that before. It's a really wonderful community. I've made friends there. I enjoy the people there. I like the coaches. Everybody's super positive and encouraging. And mostly the metrics that we talk about are things like personal bests. So I am noticing like, you know, where I'm becoming stronger and, you know, that I am faster running, and that I have good endurance and good stamina. And in that way, I'm sort of really happy with what I do there because I'm finding the sort of, like, a new strength in my body; like, what my body can do. It's not about what I look like, it is about what I am able to do with this body. I am so fast. People have actually commented on how strong and fast I am, which is sort of a nice way to talk about my body because it's not about what it looks like. It's about what it's capable of. And I like feeling that my body is as capable of awesome things as my brain is, right? I get to worry about what the noticeable non-scale victories are. And that I think is lovely because it sort of takes the physical appearance out of the fitness equation, and makes power and strength and endurance and persistence and determination the focus of the body, which makes me so much happier than the alternative. I am proud of this body in a way I never have been. It is transformative.

Resistance is powerful and, much like all of the participants, does not appear in similar ways. How we resist, where, and when is our choice. It is a journey to decide what resistance looks like and when it feels safe to speak out or react. I wanted to leave this section for Viola and Gioia's voice to come through as clearly as possible because that is one of my acts of resistance as the curator of these stories. Sometimes, they speak louder on their own.

KEY WORDS

Overdetermined; Passing; Resistance; Shame; Tokenism

QUESTIONS FOR REFLECTION AND DISCUSSION

1. Is there an element of Viola and Gioia's illustrations that you can connect to your experience? Why or why not?
2. This chapter focuses on the ways that some bodies can be characterized as in-between. Do you have any identities that you feel are living in that in-between space? How would you describe that experience?
3. The role of resistance is a challenging concept because resistance can take on many different forms—even some forms that people don't recognize. Try to come up with an example of embodied resistance that you have seen in the news or pop culture lately. How did folks use their body to resist some form of social power? How do you know?

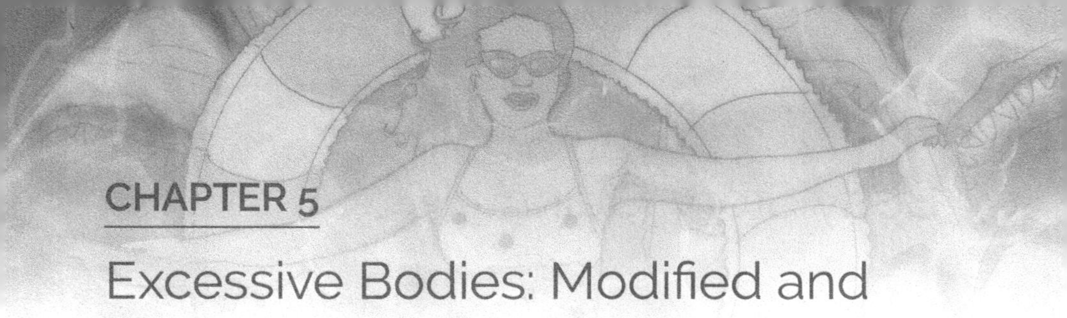

CHAPTER 5

Excessive Bodies: Modified and (Un)Natural Freaks

Body Story: Quinn

Sometimes people will just come in so hot with their question. Like, "Why do you do that to yourself? Why do you have a doughnut tattoo? Why do you have pink hair?" So, well, I don't know. "Brenda? Why do you have brown hair? That seems bland to me. Wow, you don't have tattoos? Weird. That's boring." You don't see me just saying that to these people. But, like, sometimes it's what I am thinking, right?

—Quinn

Quinn lights up a room. When we meet, her hair is pink and yellow, her bright, cartoonish tattoos on full display, and her manner has to be one of the bubbliest I have ever known. Some may not want to be described as bubbly, but this is a word Quinn used a few times in our conversation: "I feel like as much as tattoos are for myself, when people see them, I do want them to also kind of get an idea of who I am. So, my colours are very bright and, well, colourful. And also, I have some bold lines and I think that describes me—I'm very bubbly and very bright." In the last 12 years, she believes she has acquired 40–50 tattoos (she has stopped counting at this point). At 28 years old, Quinn describes herself as a "white, married, straight business owner," which she acknowledges should tick a lot of "normal" boxes, but because of the way she chooses to look, her body is a constant topic of conversation. "We live in a small, conservative town, so I get it, *but* everyone makes themselves look certain ways. Some people are totally ruthless, though, about what kind of look is appropriate for who and when."

As a woman with tattoos on her head, neck, face, and body, Quinn has given much thought to the ways her body is read. She also has a way with words that is hard to describe. We had a very interesting conversation about whether she might receive more critiques about her tattoos, piercings (there are many of those as well), and vibrant hair colours because she is seemingly rejecting elements of her white privilege.

Quinn: I see two sides of this one. So, in terms of my hair, naturally I'm a ginger and growing up it was copper top, full bloom carrot. In the summer, people would question the red because you can't even colour hair to look that way because it's so multi-dimensional. So, when I first dyed it, a lot of people were like "Oh my God, don't do that." And, like, when I first started colouring my hair, I was only making it oranger. So, yes, I think people thought I was ruining something about unique hair. But for my skin? Maybe if you just take a quick glance for sure you'd think I have beautiful porcelain skin, but then you got to go to my DNA. I am Irish and German. I am pasty as shit. When I head out, my skin is either lobster red, or maybe freckles. This version of whiteness is hard to keep porcelain. Like, it's actually not great to have it. I need SPF1000 to step into the sunshine. So, it's not "the grass is greener, folks"—obviously, I don't experience racism, but, like, it might look creamy but it's very … it's one shade off of sickly. My skin is definitely policed, though.

When we switched subjects to pop culture loves, social media followings (she describes herself as once MySpace famous), and wonderful partners, I asked her who would play her in a movie about her life. This was the list, offered with no hesitation.

Quinn: Okay. Okay. I would combine all of the following! Kristen Wiig, Zooey Deschanel, Kelly Osbourne, Cyndi Lauper, Meryl Streep … mostly I want Meryl in there because she seems like such a solid person. I aspire to be Meryl. But also, Beavis from *Beavis and Butt-Head*. Oh! And Animal from *The Muppets*. Boom!

Quinn
Damian Mellin, 2020

What if Jem and the Holograms grew up and became a kick-ass hairdresser? There is not much more to say than that. The other part of Quinn's illustration was that I wanted to pay tribute to her hunting and rural past (hence the animals) and connect it to her modern-retro style.—Damian Mellin

Body Story: Victoria

My story is last because I wanted to allow all of the other incredible women in this book to speak first. As a preface to my story, my body is privileged. As a 39-year-old, white, able-bodied, thin, cisgender woman, I recognize the space that I occupy as being one where people feel that my height is the most relevant non-conforming thing to discuss with me, and discuss it they do. My body story is one that I tell over and over again because whenever I leave my home, I am made to account for its oddity. As I have mentioned earlier, my body is tall. That's it. I am tall. People, however, like to remind me of this; they ask questions about what I do with it; children point and stare. This is my normal.

Height is something that is seen to be a privilege in society, particularly for men. Similarly, tall women are often revered. Some of the most famous beautiful women in the world (read: supermodels) are taller than average. But my body is more than normal-tall, it is odd-tall. It is even more odd-tall than people realize, but more on that later.

The average woman's height in Canada is 163.9 centimetres, or 5 feet, 4 inches (CBC 2016). I am 190.5 centimetres, or 6 feet, 3 inches. I am tall. So, who cares? Apparently, many people. Here are samples of actual questions/comments that I have been asked:

- Why are you so tall?
- How tall are you?
- Do you play basketball?
- Do you model?
- Are your parents tall?
- Have you always been this tall?
- I wish I was as tall as you!
- Do you date?
- You are blocking my view.
- You're so big.
- What kind of freak are you?

My height inspires awe. It is clear from many of the questions I receive that people are in awe of my extraordinary size. It is the spectacle of my height that is the point of discussion, but the fact that I am also beautiful encourages the dialogue further. I can say that now—"I am also beautiful"—without wanting to shirk from the statement. Vanity is supposed to be something to shun once girls become women. We are fine to dote on little girls and make them feel gorgeous and declare their beauty, but as adults? Women are to be humble and deny their own beauty, even when they fulfill the idealized versions of beautiful (which I do). I recognize that my beauty is also a privilege. It is the combination of all of me that inspires the awe and situates me as odd. It wasn't until I started doing research for this book that I realized why my body is such a spectacle. In the following chapter, I explore the ways that freak shows displayed aggrandized versions of bodies such as mine. It was both a comforting discovery and a saddening one.

As a feminist thinker, I have come to see my body as a gateway for storytelling. It is because of the constancy of comments that I receive that I was inspired to hear the body stories of other women and non-binary folks. My experience is fundamentally a gendered one. Tall men—even extraordinarily tall men—are not scrutinized in the same way as tall women. Do I date? I do. I was in a long-term relationship with the father of my daughter for 17 years. I was slightly taller than him. My partner now is more than a few inches shorter than me. He doesn't mind me sharing that he was intimidated by my height at first—he had questions of how we would work, what being with me would be like, how he would feel to be shorter than his partner. Luckily for both of us, he got over that pretty quickly.

I also have scoliosis—a curvature of the spine. When I was 13, I had surgery to correct part of it, but my spine is still quite curved to one side. Because of this curve, I appear shorter than I actually am. If doctors were to straighten out my entire spine, it would likely add two to three inches to my height. My only concerns around that would be that I would struggle to clear doors and low ceilings more than I do now—and I would need an entirely new wardrobe (which might sound silly, but clothing for my current body is already a struggle to find).

My body speaks to people in ways that make them question why they couldn't be different. The accounting for why I am this way doesn't bother me, but the physical touching of me does. Right before COVID-19 changed our patterns of public interaction, this happened:

Victoria: [*buying produce*]

White woman, in her 50s or 60s: [*comes up to me and grabs my arm*] I just wanted you to know that you are so beautiful. So tall and so beautiful.

Victoria: [*a bit stunned*] OK. [*I move to unlatch her hand from my arm*]

Her: I just really wanted you to know that you are so beautiful. I wish I was as tall as you!

Victoria: OK? Thank you.

Her: [*proceeds to ask me how tall I am and questions what I do for a living, if it relates to my height, etc.*]

This is one of those well-meaning strangers. I, like all of the interviewees in the book, ready myself for these interactions. At times, I grow weary of their frequency, but in some instances, I can feel that the interest in my body is coming from a genuine place of awe and nothing about that feels too uncomfortable (unless I am being hit on—but that's another body story altogether).

Victoria
Damian Mellin, 2020

Spoiler alert: While Victoria and I have never met in person, we had so many Zoom meetings about this book that I already knew what she looked like prior to illustration. For this illustration, I wanted to show the new guard taking over for the old guard. Victoria is pushing the dead weight of an old book away from her. The book is a classic representation of women's training books that came out during the 1940s. This outdated book, now in flames, is being pushed to the ground with one hand as the other hand is writing this book you are currently reading on a smartphone.—Damian Mellin

Body Theories: Responding to Quinn and Victoria

BIGGER, SMALLER, LOUDER, QUIETER, BROKEN, FIXED

"Freak" is a word people tend to bristle at. Its connotations are ostracizing and harsh. It is often avoided, unless used to diminish or isolate. I will never forget the times I have been labelled a freak, not by children—playground bullying tends to wash off over time—but by adults who have looked at my body with unexpected contempt. Of course, most of the encounters people have with supposed freaks beg innocent, genuinely curious questions (when they are one-off encounters). Don't forget, though: Garland-Thomson (2009) says that when extraordinary people enter into the public eye, the visual landscape enlarges. In her discussion of the visually strange, she says: "Here is the contradiction at the heart of staring, then: the extraordinary excites but alarms us; the ordinary assures but bores us" (19). We yearn for a visual spectacle to excite and challenge us, but the relationship it begins can unfold in a variety of ways. For those of us with extraordinary bodies—physically disabled, hypervisible, unusually modified, born oddities, and the like—our bodies speak stories of supposed well-meaning curiosity, but this well-meaning is historically rooted in something more sinister.

This chapter will explore the concept of the freak and the show that the freak emerges from. You will also notice that this chapter reads a bit differently than the others—my own voice comes through much more explicitly since my story is analyzed here alongside Quinn's. While this is not a common feature of much qualitative research—to include your own story alongside those of the participants—I see it as fundamental to how we, as academics and writers, are never disconnected from what we try to explore as researchers. The key elements of this chapter are disability, height, beauty, and body size because they help to frame the way that excess and binaries of normal and natural come to be. Through

Quinn's story, body modifications and the socio-cultural context that they emerge from will also be discussed.

WALKING AROUND IN PUBLIC—THE EVERYDAY FREAK SHOW

As introduced in Chapter 4, the history of the freak show and its connection to odd and awe-some bodies are undeniable. Freak shows functioned to position some bodies as unusual in order for spectators to understand themselves as "normal." As Robert Bogdan (1988) claims, "'[f]reak' is a frame of mind, a set of practices, a way of thinking about and presenting people. It is the enactment of a tradition, the performance of a stylized presentation" (3). He continues: "'Freak' is a way of thinking, of presenting, a set of practices, an institution—not a characteristic of an individual" (10). In her discussion of how she feels on display in public because of her tattoos, Quinn says: "In the town we live in, I get gawked at quite often, but when I go to bigger cities where people's bodies have much more variety, then I'm just a fly on the wall, nothing at all." To gawk at a person is to stare without abandon and without self-consciousness about the fact that you are staring. Freak shows fostered this behaviour in order to position those who looked different as spectacles to be consumed.

The characterization of "freak" exceeds individuals because it is a discourse that becomes attached to a body: freaks are not born, they are made. To provide some context, freak shows were very popular attractions in the United States in the late 19th to early 20th centuries. In the carnivalesque show, they paraded human "oddities" around and exaggerated any difference in order to sell the middle classes a spectacle to consume. As Garland-Thomson (1997) says, "[t]he freak show consequently created a 'freak,' or 'human curiosity,' from an ordinary person who had a visible physical disability or an otherwise atypical body by exaggerating the ostensible difference and the perceived distance between the viewer and the showpiece on the platform" (62). Racist narratives in the freak show fuelled concepts of the exotic Other and often framed people from non-Western nations as subhuman creatures. These bodies were also framed as exotic: "Non-Western people with demonstrable physical differences—those who were very tall, very short, without arms and legs, [conjoined] twins, and so on—were exhibited within the exotic motif through emphasis of their anomalies as well as their 'strange ways.' But many freaks who were brought from abroad had nothing 'wrong' with them physically" (Bogdan 1988, 107).

The exoticization of the Other, as we have seen in previous chapters, is a common experience for many. Part of the reason it persists is because of the social privilege that was historically created and pseudoscientifically supported for those who are not that—whatever *that* is. Freaks were and are reduced to bodies, strictly. While travelling freak shows fell out of fashion in the 1930s and 1940s—once it became clear that there were human rights violations, explicit racism and ableism, as well as blatant lies being told to the audience—we can still see the intergenerational desire to have some version of freak shows to gawk at. Television shows on the cable television channel TLC air a wide variety of shows pointing to embodied differences—particularly in terms of size, disability, and varying "extreme" modifications. Freak shows haven't left; they have adapted.

DISABLED/NON-DISABLED

Binaries limit us. There is not some easy divide between disabled and non-disabled as I seem to imply with the heading for this section. There is too much variation, too many varied experiences, too many differences. I agree. This section is strictly meant to highlight some ways to theorize dis/ability in relation to socially constructed labels and where some of these labels come from, specifically in terms of influences on our thinking about bodies that emerged from the traditional freak show era.

W. J. T. Mitchell (2001) asks: "What is it to be 'able'? What is '-ability'"? (396). As we discussed in Chapter 1, defining a disabled body is a complex process to engage in. Simi Linton (1998) states that "[t]he field of disability studies is now at a critical juncture; scholars and activists have demonstrated that disability is socially constructed to serve certain ends, but now it behooves us to demonstrate how knowledge about disability is socially produced to uphold existing practices" (4).

Disability, much like all identities, is not so much a property of bodies, but rather a cultural construct created in order to attempt to define what bodies *should* look like, be, or what they can do. Emphasizing the social construction of disability reminds us how non-disabled people or those who pass as non-disabled (as many disabilities are invisible) becomes a marker for normal—whatever normalcy is in a particular cultural moment, space, or time gets to define what non-disability can be.

Garland-Thomson (1997) succinctly explains how disability functions as a relational identity via the visual cues of appearance, where "the disabled figure operates as a code for insufficiency, contingency, and abjection—for deviant particularity—thus establishing the contours of a canonical body that garners the prerogatives and privileges of a supposedly stable, universalized normalcy" (136). As disabilities are not always conveyed through visual cues, notions of disappearances of the body, or "passing" as abled, positions a nonvisible disability as both a potential individual privilege and a form of betrayal to the disability community. The emphasis on the visual aspects of privilege is what most often comes to matter about the body.

As noted above, disabled bodies were a mainstay of traditional freak show culture, and they set the stage for the wrongness of all bodies presented in the shows. Bodily traits that were described in ableist terms served to frame disabled bodies as unintelligible in comparison to normal bodies. As we saw in Nana's body story, these frameworks of difference still serve to position some bodies as healthy, while Others are framed as sick or crazy based strictly on how they appear.

It is interesting how Nana, Kali, Alice, and I all engaged in discussions of disability as they related to our body stories, but none of us explicitly identified as disabled. I have lived with pain due to scoliosis my entire life. I wore a back brace to sleep for two years, and when my curve just kept getting worse, I had an eight-hour surgery at the age of 13 to straighten the upper half of my spine using pins, rods, and bone chips carved from my hip. A surgical scar runs down the entirety of my back, with a thick scar over my right hip that is still sensitive to the touch almost 30 years later. I have pain in my lower back most days. I can't feel parts of my shoulder blades. My scoliosis affects how I feel, how I move, and how I sleep, but not really how I look. The invisibility of my disability enables me—whether problematically or not—to identify and pass (except maybe when my scars are exposed) as non-disabled, *for now*.

We have already discussed how Nana politically chooses to not identify as disabled. Kali and I spoke at length about a wide variety of topics—she said that she was open to discuss anything, but she also said, "I have flare-ups with chronic illness, disability, but that's not a story for today." I didn't push her to explain. Alice describes her severe panic attacks and being diagnosed with body dysmorphic disorder and related to it as disabling for her, but did not identify herself as disabled in our discussion. As an identity, it seems that disability is one that is fraught with contradictions and disidentifications. In her discussion of disability, Garland-Thomson (2011) notes:

> [D]isability is a culturally fabricated narrative of the body, similar to what we understand as the fictions of race and gender. The ability/disability system produces subjects by differentiating and marking bodies. Although this comparison of bodies is ideological rather than biological, it nevertheless penetrates into the formation of culture, legitimating an unequal distribution of resources, status, and power within a biased social and architectural environment. ... Moreover, *disability* is a broad term within which cluster ideological categories as varied as *sick, deformed, crazy, ugly, old, maimed, afflicted, mad, abnormal*, or *debilitated*—all of which disadvantage people by devaluing bodies that do not conform to cultural standards. (17)

The belief in the medical commitment to healing these ideological categories is not trivial. My parents and I were told that, without medical intervention, I would not live past my 30s as my spine would eventually crush my lungs. While I am grateful for the interventions on my body as a child, I also recognize that there is an aggressive intent to fix and eliminate bodies that deviate from the norm. While these interventions likely saved my life, they also contribute to the belief that some bodies are worth saving, some bodies can function as normal-looking, and some Other bodies will always be wrong.

The desire to disidentify as disabled inhibits our ability to embrace bodies that are radically marked by their oddities. Eli Clare's (2009) discussion of *exile* is one way that perhaps we can understand this movement away from embracing disability: "It is a big word, a hard word. It implies not only loss, but a sense of allegiance and connection—however ambivalent—to the place left-behind, an attitude of mourning rather than of good riddance. It also carries with it the sense of being pushed out, compelled to leave" (35). It is my hope that this discussion of relations to non-disability do not further exile, isolate, or invisibilize the lived relations to disability that all of us live in some relation to. My goal is to highlight the ways that disability has been framed through freak show narratives and how these narratives continue to serve disabilities as embodiments that are undesirable. As Eliza Chandler (2014) says:

> As a disabled person who embodies disability with a mixture of pride and shame ... who experiences disability as communally binding, culturally important, and even a desired way of living, I "know" that there are other ways of storying disability. Lives of disability are not only made up of stories of this flavour; stories flecked with discrimination, violence and fear, stories in which disability is culturally produced as nothing more or less than a "problem in need of a solution" (Snyder & Mitchell 2002, 47). There are many of these stories but there are other ones too; stories which describe how "disability can be done differently" (Michalko & Titchkosky 2009, 1), how disability can be regarded as an ontology that is culturally important, a desired political identity, and central to the formation of "crip communities." (3)

What possibilities could be opened if we framed our bodies in relation to desiring disability (Titchkosky 2007)? For the participants in this book, this is a question not yet answered.

NOT JUST TALL; TOO TALL

Heightism, which is not a discrimination that we often hear about, is based on the belief that height is associated with differences in character or ability, which typically renders shorter people inferior to taller people (Feldman 1975). Relations of height are intensely gendered and often connected in academic writing to income possibilities. For example, Tim Gawley, Thomas Perks, and James Curtis published a study in 2009 on relations of height and authority in a Canada-wide analysis of the workplace. They concluded that the taller the men in their sample were, the more likely there existed a positive relation (in terms of merit, power, and strength) to their authority status, while shorter men seemed to attain authority, particularly in the workplace, in spite of their shorter stature. For women, these relations were not presumed. They concluded that "one might hypothesize that taller people are sometimes more healthy or fit, and, therefore, are better able to perform supervisory or managerial tasks" (Gawley, Perks, and Curtis 2009, 219). It was noted, though, that these assumptions only applied to men. In their research, there was no connection between height and authority status for women: "For tall women, then, height is not necessarily a status cue, but rather, a cue for workplace stigmatization similar to that experienced by shorter men in positions of authority" (Gawley, Perks, and Curtis 2009, 220). From their research, it seemed that there was an expectation of gendered bodies doing certain tasks based on height.

Interestingly, there is not a wide swath of academic interest in studying the gendered dynamics of height. Perhaps this is because, while height is seen as a privilege, those who deviate outside of the privileged zone are once again rendered such oddities that there are too few to study. In popular culture, TLC aired a show called *My Giant Life* (2015–2017), which followed the stories of four women who were all over 6 feet, 6 inches tall. The show was cancelled after three seasons, but the marketing of it decidedly positioned these women as social and cultural anomalies. Their representation seemed to serve the trope of the 50-foot monstrous woman quite well. TV Tropes (2020), a pop culture wiki, explains that the trope of the "giant woman" serves a few purposes:

> Because of her attractive qualities it's not uncommon to have some
> people more thrilled than terrified of her presence, which usually

ends very badly for said onlookers. If the giant female goes on a rampage it is often played for laughs or Fanservice more often than other examples of giant rampaging behemoths. It can also be used as an inversion for the classic Damsel in Distress trope, as instead of a rampaging monster kidnapping a beautiful woman, the beautiful woman is the rampaging monster, potentially kidnapping a man or, as a Shout-Out to King Kong, a regular-sized ape or monkey. (n.p.)

While I may not love the association with being an Amazon, the woman-equivalent to King Kong, or a rampaging behemoth, I think that these discussions serve to remind us how tall women are characterized in popular culture and how that can translate to how our body stories unfold.

In my own body story, I wrote about how—through researching for this book—I came across a discussion of freak shows in relation to tall women that I had not known before. Bogdan (1988) discusses various modes of freak shows, and one of those modes is the aggrandized version. In this mode, "the presentation emphasized how, with the expectation of the particular physical, mental, or behavioral condition, the freak was an upstanding, high-status person with talents of a conventional and socially prestigious nature" (108). He adds:

People who were exhibited in the aggrandized mode tended to be presented as physically normal, or even superior, in all ways except the one anomaly that was their alleged reason for fame. Emphasis, especially in the presentation of midgets and giants, was placed on the fact that a person was—as the showmen would say—"physically attractive and perfectly formed in every way, and, in no way distasteful so as to offend the audience." (109)

After reading this passage, I started to realize something that I had felt all my life but couldn't put a name to. My experiences with strangers have always been one of awe and a simultaneous and deeply rooted sense that my height disturbs them. Of course, there are specific gendered and negative associations for a woman who is taller than almost every man she meets. Men are taught to be the authority in the space, and height often affords that. When I am present, something is seen to take away from that presumed superiority. Height itself is a matter of physiology; being considered too tall, or even a giant, is something else altogether.

While shorter women may be framed as childlike (Kali, Rae, and Quinn all attest to this), taller women get placed in a unique category. I realized through reading Bogdan's work that my anomalous height was both a privilege—"You're so lucky to be tall!"—and a freak show leftover—"Why are you like this?" Other than my tallness, my embodied presentation is, as Bogdan claims, in no way distasteful. I check all the boxes—white, thin, abled, intelligent, beautiful—but I am still reminded, quite often in fact, that I belong in that freak show. I am a human curiosity, and I am not allowed to forget that. As each participant has noted along the way, our bodies are policed for their difference.

I would like to conclude this section with an apropos passage from Garland-Thomson (2011) that I came across.

> Feminist disability theory suggests that appearance and health norms often have similar disciplinary goals. For example, body braces that were developed in the 1930s, ostensibly to correct scoliosis, discipline the body to conform to dictates of both the gender and the ability systems by enforcing a standardized female form similarly to the nineteenth-century corset, which, ironically, often disabled female bodies. Although both devices normalize bodies, the brace is part of medical discourses, whereas the corset is cast as a fashion practice. (22)

This quote resonates with me because it speaks to my body, crooked spine, back brace, and femininity in a way that gives me significant pause. Through medical intervention, I have been normalized, but am not normal, but the privilege of my appearance as non-disabled allows my body to pass within the framework of awe and odd in socially pliant ways—except, of course, for that very tall woman thing.

MAKING THE NATURAL UNNATURAL: BODY MODIFICATIONS

Susie Orbach (2009) claims that "there has never been a 'natural' body: a time when bodies were untainted by cultural practices" (165). Bodies are modified from their natural form on a daily basis. We cut our hair and our nails, and often dye our hair, but we, as a society, also have entire professional fields whose work it is to permanently and surgically alter our forms for a wide array of reasons—some deemed medically necessary, some cosmetic, and some a combination of both. Of course, we also pierce our flesh and permanently draw on it through tattooing. **Body modification** refers to the "physical alternation of the body through the use of surgery, tattooing, piercing, scarification, branding, genital mutilation, implants, and other practices" (DeMello 2014, 209). These modifications can be temporary or permanent. There are many theories as to why people participate in practices of body modification, and the histories of these traditions are varied across cultures and subcultures around the world and, thus, beyond the scope of this discussion (DeMello 2014). Tattoos are also, particularly in the last few decades, very trendy. Mary Kosut (2006) refers to them as an "ironic fad"; since tattooing was once seen as deviant behaviour in Western culture, for it now to be so mainstream that it has lost most of its "edge" is, therefore, ironic. Deborah Davidson (2016) claims that tattooing is primitive and modern, a way of using our bodies as visual texts, which can function as sites of public storytelling and a tactile archive. As we know, identity formation and belonging can manifest in a variety of forms, and body modification is merely one of them.

Alice, Kali, Quinn, and I all have tattoos. (The other participants may also have tattoos, but did not feel the need to disclose them.) I actually struggle to include myself in this group because I don't feel like my membership is quite valid. Alice, Kali, and Quinn have tattoos that people see, that people talk about, that are a part of their identity. I have one tattoo, and while it is quite large, it is on my thigh, so it is not often that people see it. To me, it is personal and deeply connected to my partner and a particular (and fairly recent) time in my life. I don't see it as part of my identity, but rather as a cool, somewhat private addition. As Margo DeMello (2014) says, "[s]ince the 1960s, when tattooing began to move slowly from the margins of American society into the middle class, women have been using tattoos as a way to reclaim their bodies, and both men and women have been using tattooing as a way to highlight their sexuality" (217). Here are some of the ways that Alice and Kali discuss their tattoos and piercings:

Alice: I have some [tattoos]—one on my wrist, two on my ankles and one on my forearm that are a bit more visible than some others. The shoulder and hip are usually hidden. I've noticed a lot of people kind of ask questions or comments about that part of me. I've also had, like, fun-ly coloured hair and piercings. So, I've definitely had people kind of come into my space and ask all those things. I think the one I get the most questions on are the flock of ravens falling up or flying up my bicep. People seem to really focus in on these. Not sure why, but then a lot of people ask me about the fleur de lis on my breast. So those are kind of the two big ones that seem to attract the most attention. I tend not to go into specifics about them and not necessarily offer them up. But I do kind of answer when asked, which I'm noticing I just do with things in general. Yeah, for better for worse.

Kali: My first piercing was when I was 16. It was my belly button. I got my ears pierced at 18. I guess a lot of the time my piercings were things I did. I would pretty up things that I thought were not pretty about myself in order to sort of make me feel better about myself, so I wouldn't hate on myself so much … but my nose ring? That's different. I got the nose ring because I wanted a nose job so badly. My nose actually comes from the Irish side of my family but because I'm brown people think it's, like, an "ethnic" quote–unquote nose and it's … it's not a cute little button-like valley girl LA, little, whatever nose. And when I was younger, I was, like, "Oh God, I gotta look this way to look like the perfect white girl that I see in the advertisements." I would think to myself that I don't think I actually want a nose job but I'm being told that I should have a nose job, but I really like nose rings. So why don't I just put something on it that I think looks badass and pretty to remind me that I can be those things without slicing open my face? So, I still have my nose ring and still have my nose and I might change my mind about that for other reasons, but for now it's fine. The tattoos, those are more just, like, they … they're pieces of significance. I see it kind of like journaling. A lot of them are memorial pieces. One of them is this little narwhal on my wrist that I got at a burlesque show on a whim. [*laughs*] Not a memorial piece! I just aesthetically thought that tattoos were very, pretty good in that moment. I wanted to do memorial pieces for some people who passed away and give them something beautiful. It was kind of like a grieving process. When people ask me about them, I will explain them. Doesn't bother me.

You can see through their stories that they envision their bodies and their modifications in some ways that overlap (explaining their tattoos to those who ask), and some that don't (Kali expressing the politics inherent in her nose ring, while Alice seemingly does not want to discuss meaning at all). This is quite common—body modifications do not have to mean anything beyond the aesthetic interpretation of the viewer, or they can have deep emotional, representational, or memorial significance. Consider your relationship with body modifications—to some extent, we all participate in them: altering our hair, using makeup, piercing, and tattooing are some of the most obvious. How have these practices changed over the course of your life? Which direction do you hope they will take in the future? What is your vision for your body?

Quinn's experience with piercing, tattooing, and hair dyeing is unique in the group. Her presentation of self is highly modified. As discussed in her body story, Quinn has dozens of brightly coloured tattoos, many piercings, and unconventionally dyed hair at all times. Quinn describes how she wanted to start tattooing at 13, but didn't end up getting her first tattoo until she was 16. Her parents were supportive, but her father talked her through what she wanted and discouraged her from getting imagery she didn't seem to understand. So, she went with a ribbon on her shoulder, because she's "a little present" and she figured it is something she would like "until the end of time." Since then, she has always been thinking of new ideas, but the projects have gotten bigger and bigger; she has also left some space because she wants to get more tattoos while travelling the world.

We had lengthy discussions about her tattooing practice and aesthetic, but I asked Quinn to also describe how she started getting the tattoos that are not traditional for anyone, let alone young, feminine, petite women—specifically, the tattoos on her head and face.

Quinn: Um, those were done when I was younger. I think we would call it my quote–unquote "rebellious state" in a sense. I didn't like being limited. Example: I started tattooing my head ... oh, you have to grab the Kleenex, because I am probably going to cry ... I started to get my head tattooed when my dad passed away. He passed away from cancer. And he lost all of his hair. And, especially him being the one that supported tattoos too, it was inspired by him. [Before he died], I had an asymmetrical haircut and there was a little shady patch, and I'd colour it different colours, and then when he passed away, I wanted to get something that will really make me think of him. And so it was like this: Daddy lost all of his hair and what he went through was really tough and he probably didn't feel the best too; so, I want to try to also go through something that is, you know, kinda tough and I definitely won't feel the best. As much as I would have loved to shave my head and do all those cool support for cancer things, I'm a hairstylist; I love my hair. So, I started tattooing my head in respect to my dad.

Quinn goes on to describe how she got a little "gypsy" girl on her head, because she was always off somewhere outside building and playing and her dad would ask, "Where's my little gypsy off to now?" This was a pivotal decision in her life, but she also describes the immediate backlash that she experienced for the decision to tattoo her head.

Quinn: I was also in hair school at the time. And so I remember I came home for the holidays because I went to school out of town, got the head tattoo, went back after the holidays and my one teacher just lost it. And she was like, "Oh my God, Quinn. What are you doing?" She was like, "You are just starting your career. You're 19. Who is going to hire you with your head tattooed looking this way?" I realized in that moment that if that's your mentality and everyone else's mentality ... that if they aren't going to hire me, because I have a beautiful picture on my head, then I don't want to work there. Like, I know the weather, I know current affairs, I can listen, I'm a good listener, I'm a nice person. And if I'm a hard worker, and if all of these things can't be seen, because I have a head tattoo, then get real. I don't want to work for you, I won't work anywhere, but I'm smart—I'll figure it out. Because these things make me happy. And so that's just really what started also allowing me to push the envelope with things like that. I will always remember this one girl said to me, too: "Oh my God, Quinn. No one is ever really going to love you. You are only going to be the alternative girl with the colourful hair and the tattoos, like no one's truly going to bring you home to meet their mom." Honestly, that didn't tear me down at all. In my head, I was like, "You can go to hell. I'm going to do everything I can now, not just in spite, but to prove it to myself and to prove it to everyone that I'm talented. I'm a nice person. Go away."

Face, neck, hands, and head tattoos are public, discredible tattoos (Roberts 2016) because they are not easily coverable or disconnected from one's identity. There is still social stigma that public tattooees experience more than those who have coverable tattoos or tattoos in "normal" places. For women, these tattoo placements are both more unusual and more unacceptable, as evidenced in Quinn's discussion above. There is a gendered stigma that implies tattooing can detract from a woman's natural beauty and, therefore, also imply the tattooed woman is fiercely (and perhaps grotesquely) shunning social norms. Derek Roberts (2016) states: "Rather than being occasional expressions of the self, the tattoos of visibly tattooed renegades become an inseparable part of every frontstage and backstage self" (801). The frontstage (public persona) and personal life (backstage persona) become inextricably tied to the tattoos of those with public tattoos. I did not find it surprising that the majority of my conversation with Quinn focused on her tattoos because they are so much of who she is and how she is received by others.

BEAUTY AND THE FREAK

Beautiful women were always included in freak shows, but there had to be something amiss in order for them to be labeled "freakish." Usually, it was their extraordinary size, they were missing limbs, or they were portrayed as something other-worldly, such as a half-woman, half-animal. While being beautiful can take on a wide variety of meanings, as I said in my body story, beauty is a privilege. While it might not seem brave to announce that "I am beautiful," women are often taught to not look at ourselves in this way, because we exist to be looked at. Berger (1972) says: "In the art-form of the European nude the painters and spectator-owners were usually men and the persons treated as objects, usually women. This unequal relationship is so deeply embedded in our culture that it still structures the consciousness of many women. They do to themselves what men do to them. They survey, like men, their own femininity" (63). In relation to beauty, our body stories are more like lifelong projects that can never find completion. We can frame the goal of this project to be a myth, as Naomi Wolf did (1990); but the reality is that we can achieve it externally through the affirmations of other people, but it is the internal disbelief that makes the project unending.

To explain this idea, Bordo (2003) consistently reminds us that the body is constructed "as something apart from the true self (whether conceived as soul, mind, spirit, will, creativity, freedom …) and as undermining the best efforts of that self" (5). She goes on to say: "Through the pursuit of an ever-changing, homogenizing, elusive ideal of femininity—a pursuit without a terminus, requiring that women constantly attend to minute and often whimsical changes in fashion—female bodies become docile bodies—bodies whose forces and energies are habituated to external regulation, subjection, transformation, 'improvement'" (166). Here, Bordo is referring to the feminine body as a beauty project; a project without an end. Even when a well-meaning stranger comes up to us to say "You are beautiful," women are taught to deny this, to diminish, or to explain it as if it is not entirely true or not as true as implied.

A few years back, I remember a discussion in one of my larger classes (over a hundred students in attendance) where we were talking about beauty and the challenge for women to speak about their own beauty. I was discussing the ways that women are often taught that being humble or diminishing their own beauty is seen as more appropriate than proudly identifying that they are beautiful. I asked them how they would respond if I confidently stated that "I am smart." A few students said something to the effect of: "You are smart, so that's fine!" Then I asked them, "What if I confidently said, 'I am beautiful'? How would you respond then?" A brave male student raised his hand and said, "You shouldn't say that. It makes you seem too vain. Like you are full of yourself and not a good person." I remember some nods from other male students, but what I mostly remember were the nods from the female students. There were so many. After a pause, one female student put up her hand and quietly said something akin to: "But you are beautiful; so I don't get it?" The same male student then said, "She is. That's the point!" It was clear then that it is because I am seen as beautiful that naming myself that way must imply a deficit of character. I fail at being beautiful because I shouldn't be the one naming myself as that; according to patriarchal expectations, that determination must come from outside sources.

While each participant spoke about beauty in some way, Kali is the participant who spoke most openly about beauty. She discusses her desire to use lip fillers and explains it as both a response to social pressure and an internal urge to want to change.

Kali: The fillers? It wasn't something where we all feel pressure from the beauty industry or from comments people say, but I do think it is a vulnerability versus understanding the systems. Yeah. I'm a woman like anyone else who feels insecure and vulnerable. But I also know myself and I like my brown skin now even though I used to hate it. I like my brown eyes now even though I used to want blue eyes. But I never liked my tiny upper lip. I always wanted that full lip. Like, I can remember being a child and seeing other girls in my class who had fuller upper lips and I would think to myself about how cool that was. I want that, you know, right away, I was wanting that to happen. And so, then I realized that now I can have it. And if suddenly I can't have fillers tomorrow, I'll still be a complete person without it, but if I can access it, then that's what I want.

Some may consider this desire to have fuller lips as being duped by a patriarchal system that says beauty looks a certain way, and that Kali should do whatever she can to participate and achieve this look. This, however, is too simplistic. Kali is not a victim. She is using her agency to work within the structures of society and make choices that she believes will ultimately allow her to achieve a look that she has desired since childhood. In discussing women's aesthetic beauty choices, Dolezal (2015) says, "[R]ather than being duped and deluded, they are often fully aware of the coercive and sometimes harmful nature of beauty norms, but at the same time, however, are unwilling or unable to give up the social capital that conforming to these norms affords" (144).

At one point in our discussion, Quinn noted: "People think I have beautiful skin, beautiful eyes ... and I can tell that they wonder why I cover myself in tattoos and have this bright, candy-coloured hair. (I can also tell they think this since they tell me about it!) I just don't care anymore ... No, it's not that I don't care ... I do this for me, but ... I don't know. It's so super complicated." Berger (1972) argues that "a woman must continually watch herself. She is almost continually accompanied by her own image of herself. ... And so she comes to consider the surveyor and the surveyed within her as the two constituent yet always distinct elements of her identity as a woman" (46). Quinn's contradiction above speaks directly to the ways that women are forced to grapple with the comments and beliefs of others in relation to their beauty. Berger goes on to say: "One might simplify this by saying: men act and women appear. Women watch themselves being looked at. This determines not only most relations between men and women but also the relation of women to themselves" (47). The challenge to identify oneself as beautiful is difficult for all genders, but for women, the elusive ideals of beauty often remain elusive every time they look in a mirror for the entirety of their lives. This is not a vanity problem; it is a patriarchal one.

Quinn knows that she will be stared at, as do I. As do all participants in this book. The question, perhaps, isn't if we will be stared at, but how we will be stared at. At times, it is because we are inspiring the awe of other people; other times we are being relegated to odd *mis*fits. Navigating feelings about the experience of those realities seems to be an ongoing process for all of us, as are our choices about how and if we will respond. This is clearly a process that our bodies and reflections will undertake for the entirety of our lives.

KEY WORDS

Body modification; Freak; Heightism

QUESTIONS FOR REFLECTION AND DISCUSSION

1. Has there ever been a time that you felt like a social misfit or freak? Did/ do you desire this feeling?

2. Why are some parts of our bodies seen as "okay" to modify and other parts stigmatized? For example, Quinn's discussion of face and head tattoos. Do you see this stigma as something that will shift over time?

3. While Damian and Victoria have never met in person, he based his illustration of her off a Zoom call where they saw each other. What do you think of the strategy of him not seeing the other participants? Do you think it was a meaningful exercise for him to envision Quinn, etc. and create their image from their body stories? Why or why not?

CHAPTER 6

Bodies and Their Stories

Figure 6.1. Eight Women
Damian Mellin, 2020

I am always hesitant to write a formal conclusion. While I believe that there are areas I want to further reflect on, I feel that this book deserves to be left a bit open-ended. I want to leave a space for you to apply these ideas in your own way. You will see after some thoughts on online bodies and pedagogical bodies, as well as some final thoughts from the participants, that there is a space for your own body story, as well as one for an illustration or whatever else serves your interest. This is mostly because the stories that you have read throughout this book are just a handful among millions. They each matter, they each teach us things, and they would each be told differently if our conversations happened a year ago, today, or a year from now. Our bodies change, our encounters in public change, and our perceptions of ourselves change.

LIVING ONLINE

When I originally conceived of this book, I had assumed that much more of it would be devoted to our online bodies and identities. As someone who teaches communication and media studies, this is something I had hoped would be quite prevalent. Interestingly, when I asked the participants about their identities online, it was a challenging topic as there was little consistency about their use of social media to express themselves. The most consistent element was a deep ambivalence about how to present oneself and interact with others when opinions and public scrutiny proliferate, judgements are quick, and discriminations seem to be around many corners of virtual interactions. Of course, there were positive experiences of connections and community, but it was not a space that many of the body stories drifted toward. I wonder what responses those questions would glean now. After nearly two years of so many of us living primarily online for work, schooling, and social connections, our virtual bodies have taken on new meanings. As I noted in Chapter 1, while our interactions in public have changed with social distancing and mask-wearing, our interactions in public will undoubtedly return to some semblance of pre-pandemic normalcy—perhaps they already have. Our bodies in public will take on new meanings, but also familiar ones. Our bodies online, however, may be the ones that are just starting to be newly realized. Who we are, in relation to how we create and recreate ourselves online, is something that the vast majority of society had not had to thoughtfully consider, until now. If there is a follow-up to this book, I am certain it will connect to how we live online and how we conceive of our embodiments in virtual spaces.

BODIES AS PEDAGOGICAL

I hope that this book has helped to make clear how our bodies can be pedagogical. **Pedagogy** refers to the method and practice of teaching, especially as an academic subject or theoretical concept. So, why are bodies pedagogical? Well, every day they teach us how to feel both physically and emotionally. For those open to learning, the body can be a conduit of these teachings. Bodies teach us how (and perhaps how not) to interact with other people. Bodies teach us their own limits, how to heal, and help us to navigate all of the possibilities of life. As you can see from the body stories in this book, bodies have taught the participants key lessons of who and how they want to be in relation to how others see and treat them. Many times, throughout this book, the participants discussed how they would often try to teach well-meaning strangers about what just made them uncomfortable, or how experiences with strangers inspired them to make social and political changes via their work and education. The learning that can happen through embodied moments is extraordinary.

> Appearances, as we have seen, are much "more than just surfaces." They are intimately linked to how one values and sees oneself, and furthermore to one's social worth and position within a social group. This is especially the case for women, as how they look and present themselves affects how they are treated and their chances for success in various aspects of their lives. (Dolezal 2015, 107)

While I may have led the conversations with the participants, these stories were only slightly below the surface. Body stories are in all of us, as they reflect the legacies of our identities, choices, and meanings we imbue into the world around us. There are so many instances of public scrutiny that we all shrug off, but once we give space to discuss them, we can then realize the impact that they have had on how we conceive of ourselves and the choices that we want to make about these inter- actions going forward.

I described the resistance that appears in this book as fierce, but not because it is necessarily angry or aggressive (of course, it still can be!). Rather, I am using the term in the more contemporary usage with which I am most familiar. As I mentioned in Chapter 4, if someone is fierce it commonly means that they possess a great, intense, powerful, and/or beautiful quality to them. I often call my daughter fierce because of the intensity of her spirit and the attitude that she approaches life with. This form of fierceness is brave, quiet, loud, blatant, subtle, and inspiring. It is all of these things. My hope is that you take this idea of what resistance can mean from this book. We can resist any form of public scrutiny that tries to diminish us. We can resist being talked to in a way that we don't like. We can resist feeling like we always have to be polite. We can resist engaging with those who don't make us feel safe. We can express our bodies in the ways that we want. We can connect with those who make us feel powerful. This is fierceness.

THEY WANT YOU TO KNOW ...

At the end of each interview, I asked the participants if there was any- thing more that they would like you to know. I feel it is appropriate to end with their words. Here is what they each said:

Nana: I actually just want you to know that I am grateful for the ability to tell people about my life. To know that work like this exists. I find this inspiring and lovely and it makes me interested in joining communities of people who have an interest in the lives and bodies of others. Knowing that people will read this and perhaps learn something? It is so meaningful.

Rae: I would want people to think twice about how they speak to those they don't know. I know that I do it more now. I know that we follow our ideals in society and want to reach out to someone who has maybe lost weight or something and say, "Oh, you look so beautiful, so good," but maybe in reality they are sick. Maybe they are on medication. There could be a whole list of reasons why they now look this way. Instead of saying they look great, maybe we all need to be better at saying, "How are you?" Or even describing things that aren't so much attributed to physical attributes, but saying, "You look really happy," or "You're thriving." It is such a better way to approach people and such a good reminder for all of us.

Kali: I guess I just wish to convey how important it is to start from a general principle of being kind to people. I do think it is important for us to have certain values about how you treat others, and I am not even just referring to avoiding commenting on people's weight or body, but the general principle of what kindness means. What does it look like to approach a stranger from a perspective of kindness? Do they need to hear what you are planning to say? What is your intention? And, like, is it selfishly motivated? And I have definitely learned these lessons more and more as I have gotten older. I learn from people all the time about how to check my privilege in a situation, so I think that is something to really value. Question, question, question.

Alice: A lesson I have learned is that I tend to not ask people questions. Or at least, do my best not to. Obviously, people slip up every now and then, but for the most part I kind of just try to take people at face value and work with the information they give me or are willing to give me. I struggle when people feel entitled to information. Just let them share what they want.

Viola: I hope that white guys read this and learn they shouldn't be cringy. [*laughs*]

Gioia: As I have gotten older, I have learned how to sort of step outside my body and still be present. It has taken almost 40 years and I am still building up my self-worth, but this body is a project worth working on.

Quinn: The last thing I'd like people to take away from this is to be kind to people. Because, seriously, I am like a duck, I might look poised and everything on top [of the water], but these feets are flapping under the water. And I think that's most of us. I might look calm. I might exude confidence with my pink hairs and my tattoos. I might seem like I don't care. But I do care. Not so much like where you can't have your opinion because that's a you thing. We're all entitled to it. But, like, just don't be shitty to people. Because, like, most of us are already having a shitty time. And, like, if we're choosing, especially if we're choosing to look certain ways, it's because it's making us happy. So, we don't need you to shit on our parade. Be happy. Share in the happy!

I want to close with prioritizing their voices, as I have so often tried to do. It is their experiences that have encouraged us to think about gender, staring, sexuality, race, shame, disability, body modifications, and appearances, among many other topics. As we have seen, in difficult moments, we may feel like our bodies belong to the opinions of other people; that we understand them strictly through the lens of the stranger's stare—making us feel odd. In a global pandemic, our bodies become our conduit of health, sometimes fraught with worry and uncertainty. But, in separate moments, we reclaim our bodies as our own; as powerful, beautiful, and so extraordinary that they can inspire our own awe.

KEY WORD

Pedagogy

Storying Your Body

Here is a space for your own body story. Here are some questions for reflection to get you started:

- Have you ever had someone come up to you in public to ask you something about how you look? What did they say? How did you respond? How did it make you feel? Why was this encounter memorable?
- Have you altered your body because of other people's comments?
- If you were to describe your personal style, what would you say?
- How would you describe your online identity? What kinds of images of yourself do you share and why?
- How does your offline identity differ from your online identity?
- How would your friends describe you?
- Who should play you in a movie about your life?
- What is your favourite part of your body? Why?
- How do you express your gender?
- Are there any assumptions that people make of you based on how you look?
- What five words would you use to describe your personality?
- What five words would you use to describe your appearance?

_____

_____

_____

_____

_____

_____

_____

_____

BODY ILLUSTRATION

Here, you could use this space to draw yourself, have someone else draw you, or draw one of the participants in the way that you envisioned them.

Appendix

QUESTIONS FOR DISCUSSION AND REFLECTION

In this section, I wanted to create a space that gives readers the opportunity for reflection that reading, learning, and thinking about bodies can inspire. These questions can be used in a classroom, talked about over dinner, or written out in a journal—any of the places learning and reflection can happen. The questions start from a pragmatic frame of reflection on the main topics in the book and then shift to a more reflexive element of questioning your own embodied experiences.

1. Why does storytelling about our bodies matter? What are the limits of these stories?
2. What is your response to the art style? If you read the body stories before looking at the illustrations, how did you imagine each person? How did the artist's vision differ from yours?
3. Which chapter most connected with your experience? Why?
4. Which chapter felt most disconnected from your own body story? How did that make you feel?
5. Which story taught you the most?
6. Which chapter was the most challenging for you to read? Why?
7. When you have received a comment about how you look, how did that make you feel? What is memorable about that experience? Why do you find it memorable?
8. When people stare at you in public, what do you think it is that they are curious about?
9. When you stare at other people in public, what is it that might catch your attention? What are you trying to discover?
10. Recall a specific experience where you stared at someone. What was it that you were trying to discover? When or how did you decide the staring should end?

11. Has reading this book impacted the way you think about bodies? Staring? Asking questions of other people?

12. What do you think is most valuable about listening to body stories?

Glossary

Ability is a socially constructed signifier for normal bodies; whatever is considered a "normal body" in any particular cultural moment, space, or time will indicate to a culture what it means to have an "able" body.

Ally is an identity that individuals use when they actively and consistently practise reflection on what they do or say as a person in a position of privilege and power, while they actively work in solidarity with marginalized groups.

Body—The body is a biological, material, and symbolic form of a person.

Body modification is the intentional altering of the human body or appearance.

Body stories are the narratives that we tell about our bodies. These stories can include the physical, social, and emotional experiences and interpretations of our bodies.

Cisgender people have a gender identity or gender expression that has not changed from the gender that they were assigned at birth.

Colonization is the large-scale process of invading nations, assuming control of Indigenous territory, and applying external systems of law, government, and religion as a process of assimilation and/or genocide to the Indigenous peoples. The Canadian nation was created through a process of colonization.

Disability is a socially constructed identity that can be defined as a representation, a cultural interpretation of bodily difference, and a comparison of bodies that structure social relations and institutions.

Embodiment usually refers to how the body is involved in social interactions that create meanings. These meanings are based on how our physical experiences—through bodily form, gaze, gesture, posture, facial expression, and movement—shape the form of our interactions with social and cultural environments.

Exotic—The concept of the exotic is the characterization of a person or material object that originated in or is characteristic of a non-Western country.

Feminism is a movement that aims to end sexism, sexist exploitation, and oppression.

Fetishized—To be fetishized is an active process of being positioned as a sexualized object of desire, intrigue, or worship.

Freak refers to a person who is considered physically "abnormal" or transformed from an extreme body modification.

Gender refers to the socially constructed roles, behaviours, activities, and attributes that relate to understandings of masculinities, femininities, and non-binary embodiments in every society.

Heightism is the discrimination against people based on height. It refers to the discrimination against people whose height is not within the normative expectations for height in a population.

Heteronormativity refers to a belief and a set of cultural-institutional practices that enforce heterosexuality as the dominant, essential, preferred, and "natural" norm.

Homonormativity encourages 2SLGBTQIA+ people to attempt to mimic heterosexuality and all of its created characteristics and assumptions.

Identity is a relational process through which we understand ourselves, others, and groups at any given time, in any given place. Identities include our gender, race, class, ability, sexuality, religion, nation, and other aspects of our personal relationships to one another.

Intersectionality refers to how biological, social, and cultural categories such as gender, race, class, ability, sexual orientation, and other axes of identity interact and intersect on multiple and often simultaneous levels.

Normal is a relation where someone or something is deemed to be conforming to a standard that is "typical" or "expected."

Oppression happens when systemic forces limit the opportunities of people who are caught within them. Oppression occurs along socially significant lines, such as gender, race, sexuality, and nation.

It is a web of systemic forces that shape the world into its current structures.

Overdetermined—To be overdetermined refers to how we account for or create meaning for something due to multiple causes or with more conditions than are necessary.

Passing is the ability of a person to be regarded as a member of an identity, such as culture or community, different from their own, which may include gender, race, class, sexuality, age, and/or disability. Passing may result in social power or privilege.

Patriarchy can be defined as a system of societal oppression where men and masculinity hold dominant positions of power and influence, specifically in terms of political and social institutions.

Pedagogy refers to the method and practice of teaching, especially as an academic subject or theoretical concept.

Power is used in a variety of ways to mean a relation of social, cultural, economic, material, and physical domination.

Privilege is a relation of power that positions certain bodies as having unearned advantages that are systemically created and culturally reinforced.

Public scrutiny is when a person or thing is being watched, observed, and assessed—both explicitly and implicitly—by other people.

Queer is an umbrella term that can be as open-ended and inclusive as possible. Queerness is both an orientation and a community for those on the 2SLGBTQIA+ spectrum.

Race is a socially constructed category that serves to separate people based on practices of exclusion and oppression in relation to ancestry, appearance, and social location.

Racialization is the process that causes relationships, social practices, or groups to have racial meanings in society.

Resistance can mean to immediately refuse to accept or comply with something, but it can also mean to bear witness, to react passively and have that experience potentially spark future decision-making and social change.

Sex can refer to the physiological classifications of biological bodies or the practice of engaging in sexual activity and/or intercourse.

Sex critical is a characterization for someone who does not rely solely on the idea that people must be either sex positive or sex negative, but rather prioritizes critical thinking about the concept of "sexuality."

Sex positive—To be sex positive refers to having or promoting an open, accepting, and progressive attitude toward sexual behaviour and sexuality.

Sexotic characterizes the intersection between processes of sexualization and exoticization in terms of alleged differences in the sexual drive, attitudes toward sexuality, and sexual behavior, which construct the supposed desirability of the exotic quality.

Sexuality is a social category that defines our sexual interests, desires, and intimacies. Sexuality has been used as an element of social control to deem some desires as "normal" and others as "wrong."

Shame is a powerful emotion of humiliation, distress, and self-loathing that can be brought on through a wide variety of external sources.

Social constructionism is a theory of knowledge that examines how social beings work together to construct understandings of the world, and these understandings—based on systems of representations— then form the basis for shared assumptions about life.

Stigma is the disapproval of, or discrimination against, a person based on perceivable social and embodied characteristics that serve to distinguish them from other members of a society and "spoil" their identity.

Tokenism is the process whereby people of various identities are asked or made to "stand in" as the singular person or limited group of people with knowledge and expertise in order to provide legitimacy.

Transgender people have a gender identity or gender expression that differs from the gender that they were assigned at birth.

White supremacy is the belief that white people are superior to other races. Further, it refers to a social system in which white people have social privileges over other racialized groups, on both a collective and individual level, despite legal equality.

Women is a social category that includes all people who identify as women, whether they were assigned that designation at birth or if they moved toward that category later.

2SLGBTQIA+ is an acronym for those who are a part of the queer community. The acronym stands for, but is not limited to, Two-Spirit, lesbian, gay, bisexual, transgender, queer, questioning, intersex, asexual, agender, androgynous, genderfluid, genderqueer, bigender, pansexual, and so on.

References

Agustín, Laura. 2007. *Sex at the Margins: Migration, Labour Markets and the Rescue Industry*. London: Zed Books.

Ahmed, Sara. 2004. *The Cultural Politics of Shame*. Edinburgh: Edinburgh University Press.

Albury, Kath. 2017. "Heterosexual Casual Sex: From Free Love to Tinder." In *The Routledge Companion to Media, Sex and Sexuality*, edited by Clarissa Smith and Feona Attwood, 81–90. New York: Routledge.

Allen, Louisa. 2005. *Sexual Subjects: Young People, Sexuality and Education*. Basingstoke, UK: Palgrave Macmillan.

Allen, Louisa, and Mary Lou Rasmussen. 2017. *The Palgrave Handbook of Sexuality Education*. Basingstoke, UK: Palgrave Macmillan.

Altamirano-Jiménez, Isabel, and Nathalie Kermoal. 2016. "Introduction: Indigenous Women and Knowledge." In *Living on the Land: Indigenous Women's Understanding of Place*, edited by Nathalie Kermoal and Isabel Altamirano-Jiménez, 3–17. Edmonton, AB: AU Press.

Anzaldúa, Gloria. 2001. "La Conciencia de la Mestiza: Towards a New Consciousness." In *Feminism and 'Race,'* edited by Kum-Kum Bhavnani, 17–32. New York and Oxford: Oxford University Press. Original edition, 1987.

Attwood, Feona. 2018. *Sex Media*. Cambridge, MA: Polity.

Baum, Bruce. 2006. *The Rise and Fall of the Caucasian Race: A Political History of Racial Identity*. New York: New York University Press.

Benedict, Elizabeth, ed. 2015. "Introduction." In *Me, My Hair, and I: Twenty-Seven Women Untangle an Obsession*. New York: Workman.

Berger, John. 1972. *Ways of Seeing*. London: Penguin.

Bogdan, Robert. 1988. *Freak Show: Presenting Human Oddities for Amusement and Profit*. Chicago: University of Chicago Press.

Bordo, Susan. 2003. *Unbearable Weight: Feminism, Western Culture, and the Body*. Berkeley and Los Angeles: University of California Press.

Butler, Judith. 1993. *Bodies That Matter: On the Discursive Limits of "Sex."* New York: Routledge.

———. 2005. *Giving an Account of Oneself*. New York: Fordham University Press.

Camaiti Hostert, Anna. 2007. *Passing: A Strategy to Dissolve Identities and Remap Differences*. Translated by Christine Marciasini. Cranbury, NJ: Fairleigh Dickinson University Press.

Casper, Monica J., and Lisa Jean Moore. 2009. *Missing Bodies: The Politics of Visibility*. New York: New York University Press.

CBC. 2016. "Canadians Still Getting Taller, but Not as Fast as Others." *CBC*, July 26, 2016. https://www.cbc.ca/news/health/height-growth-canada-1.3695398.

Chandler, Eliza. 2014. "Disability and the Desire for Community." PhD diss., University of Toronto. https://tspace.library.utoronto.ca/bitstream/1807/68432/1/Chandler_Eliza_201411_PhD_thesis.pdf

Chateauvert, Melinda. 2013. *Sex Workers Unite: A History of the Movement From Stonewall to Slutwalk*. Boston, MA: Beacon Press.

Cho, Sumi, Kimberlé Crenshaw, and Leslie McCall. 2013. "Toward a Field of Intersectionality Studies: Theory, Applications, and Praxis." *Signs* 38 (4): 785–810. https://doi.org/10.1086/669608.

Clare, Eli. 2001. "Stolen Bodies, Reclaimed Bodies: Disability and Queerness." *Public Culture* 13 (3): 359–65. https://doi.org/10.1215/08992363-13-3-359.

———. 2009. *Exile & Pride: Disability, Queerness and Liberation*. Cambridge, MA: South End.

Cole, Desmond. 2020. *The Skin We're In: A Year of Black Resistance and Power*. Toronto: Doubleday.

Cote-Meek, Sheila. 2014. *Colonized Classrooms: Racism, Trauma and Resistance in Post-Secondary Education*. Black Point, NS: Fernwood.

Creese, Gillian. 2019. "'Where Are You From?' Racialization, Belonging and Identity among Second-Generation African-Canadians." *Ethnic and Racial Studies* 42 (9): 1476–94. https://doi.org/10.1080/01419870.2018.1484503.

Crenshaw, Kimberlé. 1989. "Demarginalizing the Intersection of Race and Sex: A Black Feminist Critique of Antidiscrimination Doctrine, Feminist Theory and Antiracist Politics." *University of Chicago Legal Forum* 1 (8): 139–67.

Dabiri, Emma. 2019. *Don't Touch My Hair*. Great Britain: Penguin Random House.

Davidson, Deborah, ed. 2016. "Introducing the Tattoo Project." In *The Tattoo Project: Commemorative Tattoos, Visual Culture, and the Digital Archive*, 1–17. Toronto: Canadian Scholars.

DeMello, Margo. 2014. *Body Studies: An Introduction*. New York: Routledge.

Dolezal, Luna. 2015. *The Body and Shame: Phenomenology, Feminism, and the Socially Shaped Body*. London: Lexington Books.

Downing, Lisa. 2012. "What Is Sex Critical and Why Should We Care About It?" *Musings of a Curmudgeonly Sexuality Studies Scholar*. Accessed June 12, 2021. http://sexcritical.co.uk/2012/07/27/what-is-sex-critical-and-why-should-we-care-about-it/.

Dyer, Richard. 1997. *White*. New York: Routledge.

Egan, Danielle R. 2013. *Becoming Sexual: A Critical Appraisal of the Sexualization of Girls*. Cambridge, MA: Polity.

Fausto-Sterling, Anne. 2000. *Sexing the Body: Gender Politics and the Construction of Sexuality*. New York: Basic Books.

Feldman, Stefan D. 1975. "The Presentation of Shortness in Everyday Life—Height and Heightism in American Society." In *Lifestyles: Diversity in American Society* (2nd ed.). 437–44. Boston, MA: Little, Brown and Company.

Foucault, Michel. 1984. "Nietzsche, Genealogy, History." In *The Foucault Reader*, edited by Paul Rabinow, 145–72. New York: Pantheon Books. Original edition, 1971.

———. 1990. *The History of Sexuality: An Introduction* (Vol. 1). New York: Random House. Original edition, 1978.

———. 2007. *Security, Territory, Population: Lectures at the College de France 1977–1978*. Translated by Graham Burchell. Edited by Michel Senellart. New York: Palgrave Macmillan.

Frankenberg, Ruth. 1993. *White Women, Race Matters: The Social Construction of Whiteness*. Minneapolis, MN: University of Minnesota Press.

Fritsch, Kelly. 2019. "Ramping Up Canadian Disability Culture." In *The Spaces and Places of Canadian Popular Culture*, edited by Victoria Kannen and Neil Shyminsky, 265–72. Toronto: Canadian Scholars' Press.

Garland-Thomson, Rosemarie. 1997. *Extraordinary Bodies: Figuring Physical Disability in American Culture and Literature*. New York: Columbia University Press.

———. 2009. *Staring: How We Look*. New York: Oxford.

———. 2011. "Integrating Disability, Transforming Feminist Theory." In *Feminist Disability Studies*, edited by Kim Q. Hall, 13–47. Bloomington, IN: Indiana University Press.

Gawley, Tim, Thomas Perks, and James Curtis. 2009. "Height, Gender, and Authority Status at Work: Analyses for a National Sample of Canadian Workers." *Sex Roles* 60: 208–22. https://doi.org/10.1007/s11199-008-9520-5.

Gieseking, Jen Jack, and William Mangold, eds. 2014. "Introduction." In *The People, Place, and Space Reader.* http://peopleplacespace.org/toc/introduction/.

Goffman, Erving. 1963. *Stigma: Notes on the Management of Spoiled Identity.* New York: Simon & Schuster.

Golden, Marita. 2015. "My Black Hair." In *Me, My Hair, and I: Twenty-Seven Women Untangle an Obsession*, edited by Elizabeth Benedict, 19–33. New York: Workman.

Gonzalez-Sobrino, Bianca, and Devon R. Goss. 2019. "Exploring the Mechanisms of Racialization Beyond the Black-White Binary." *Ethnic and Racial Studies* 42 (4): 505–10. https://doi.org/10.1080/01419870.2018.1444781.

Grosz, Elizabeth. 1994. *Volatile Bodies: Toward a Corporeal Feminism.* Bloomington, IN: Indiana University Press.

Hall, Stuart. 1996. "Who Needs Identity?" In *Questions of Cultural Identity*, edited by Stuart Hall and Paul du Gay. London: Sage.

hooks, bell. 2000. *Feminism Is for Everybody: Passionate Politics.* Cambridge, MA: South End.

Ingraham, Chrys. 2017. "Heterosexuality: It's Just Not Natural!" In *Sex, Gender, and Sexuality: The New Basics. An Anthology,* edited by Abby L. Ferber, Kimberly Holocomb, and Tre Wentling, 73–81. New York: Oxford University Press.

Jobin, Shalene. 2016. "Double Consciousness and Nehiyawak (Cree) Perspectives." In *Living on the Land: Indigenous Women's Understanding of Place*, edited by Nathalie Kermoal and Isabel Altamirano-Jiménez, 39–58. Edmonton, AB: AU Press.

Kannen, Victoria. 2013. "Pregnant, Privileged and PhDing: Exploring Embodiments in Qualitative Research." *Journal of Gender Studies* 22 (2): 178–91. https://doi.org/10.1080/09589236.2012.745681.

Kosut, Mary. 2006. "An Ironic Fad: The Commodification and Consumption of Tattoos." *The Journal of Popular Culture* 39 (6): 1035–48. https://doi.org/10.1111/j.1540-5931.2006.00333.x.

Kroeger, Brooke. 2003. *Passing: When People Can't Be Who They Are.* New York: Public Affairs.

Linton, Simi. 1998. *Claiming Disability: Knowledge and Identity*. New York: New York University Press.

Mack, Ashley Noel, and Tiara R. Na'puti. 2019. "'Our Bodies Are Not Terra Nullius': Building a Decolonial Feminist Resistance to Gendered Violence." *Women's Studies in Communication* 42 (3): 347–70. https://doi.org/10.1080/07491 409.2019.1637803.

Mahtani, Minelle. 2001. "'I'm a Blonde-Haired, Blue-Eyed Black Girl': Mapping Mobile Paradoxical Spaces among Multiethnic Women in Toronto, Canada." In *Rethinking 'Mixed Race,'* edited by David Parker and Miri Song, 173–90. London: Pluto Press.

McIntosh, Peggy. 1990. "White Privilege: Unpacking the Invisible Knapsack." *Independent School*, 31–36. Excerpt available at https://precollege-summer.uconn.edu/wp-content/uploads/sites/264/2018/07/McIntosh_WhitePrivilegeKnapsack-19901.pdf.

Merriam-Webster. 2020. "Exotic." Accessed June 12, 2021. https://www.merriam-webster.com/dictionary/exotic#:~:text=1%20%3A%20very%20different%2C%20strange%2C,from%20Merriam%2DWebster%20on%20exotic.

Mitchell, W. J. T. 2001. "Seeing Disability." *Public Culture* 13 (3): 391–97. https://doi.org. /10.1215/08992363-13-3- 391.

Nixon, Paul G., and Isabel K. Düsterköft. 2018. *Digital Empowerment: Whose Empowerment? On the Limits of Gender and Sexuality in the Digital Age*. Oxon, UK: Routledge.

Orbach, Susie. 2009. *Bodies*. New York: Picador.

Orenstein, Peggy. 2016. *Girls & Sex: Navigating the Complicated New Landscape*. New York: HarperCollins.

Parker, David, and Miri Song, eds. 2001. "Introduction." In *Rethinking 'Mixed Race,'* 1–22. London: Pluto Press.

Puwar, Nirmal. 2004. *Space Invaders: Race, Gender and Bodies Out of Place*. New York: Oxford International.

Ringrose, Jessica, and Laura Harvey. 2015. "Boobs, Back-off, Six Packs and Bits: Mediated Body Parts, Gendered Reward, and Sexual Shame in Teens' Sexting Images." *Continuum: Journal of Media & Cultural Studies* 29 (2): 205–17. https://doi.org/10.1080/10304312.2015.1022952.

Roberts, Derek. 2016. "Using Dramaturgy to Better Understand Contemporary Western Tattoos." *Sociology Compass* 10 (9).

Ross, Loretta. 2017. "Reproductive Justice as Intersectional Feminist Activism." *Souls: A Critical Journal of Black Politics, Culture, and Society* 19 (3): 286–314. https://doi.org/10.1080/10999949.2017.1389634.

RuPaul's Drag Race. 2009–Present. USA: Logo TV and VH1.

Satzewich, Vic, and Nikolaos Liodakis. 2013. *"Race" and Ethnicity in Canada.* 3rd ed. Don Mills, ON: Oxford University Press.

Schaper, Ulrike, Magdalena Beljan, Pascal Eitler, Christopher Ewing, and Benno Gammer. 2020. "Sexotic: The Interplay between Sexualization and Exoticization." *Sexualities* 23 (1–2): 114–26.

Seshandri-Crooks, Kalpana. 2000. *Desiring Whiteness: A Lacanian Analysis of Race.* New York: Routledge.

Solinger, Rickie. 2019. *Pregnancy and Power: A History of Reproductive Politics in the United States.* New York: New York University Press.

Sommer, Robert. 2007. *Personal Space: The Behavioral Basis of Design.* Bristol: Bosko Books.

Titchkosky, Tanya. 2003. *Disability, Self, and Society.* Toronto: University of Toronto Press.

———. 2007. *Reading and Writing Disability Differently: The Textured Life of Embodiment.* Toronto: University of Toronto Press.

TV Tropes. n.d. "Giant Woman." *TV Tropes.* Accessed November 7, 2020. https://tvtropes.org/pmwiki/pmwiki.php/Main/GiantWoman.

Tuhiwai Smith, Linda. 2012. *Decolonizing Methodologies: Research and Indigenous Peoples.* 2nd ed. London & New York: Zed Books.

Turner, Bryan S. 1984. *The Body and Society: Explorations in Social Theory.* New York: Basil Blackwell.

Waring, Chandra D. L. 2013. "'They See Me as Exotic ... That Intrigues Them': Gender, Sexuality and the Racially Ambiguous Body." *Race, Gender & Class* 20 (3/4): 299–317.

Warner, Michael. 2002. "Publics and Counterpublics." *Public Culture* 14 (1): 49–90. https://doi.org/10.1215/08992363-14-1-49.

Weedon, Chris. 1987. *Feminist Practice and Poststructuralist Theory.* New York: Basil Blackwell.

Wolf, Naomi. 1990. *The Beauty Myth: How Images of Beauty Are Used Against Women.* New York: Harper Perennial.